Future Asia

Future Asia

The New Gold Rush
in the East

Rajiv Biswas

With best wishes

palgrave
macmillan

First published 2013 by
PALGRAVE MACMILLAN

Palgrave Macmillan in the UK is an imprint of Macmillan Publishers Limited, registered in England, company number 785998, of Houndmills, Basingstoke, Hampshire RG21 6XS.

Palgrave Macmillan in the US is a division of St Martin's Press LLC, 175 Fifth Avenue, New York, NY 10010.

Palgrave Macmillan is the global academic imprint of the above companies and has companies and representatives throughout the world.

Palgrave® and Macmillan® are registered trademarks in the United States, the United Kingdom, Europe and other countries

ISBN: 978–1–137–02721–4

This book is printed on paper suitable for recycling and made from fully managed and sustained forest sources. Logging, pulping and manufacturing processes are expected to conform to the environmental regulations of the country of origin.

A catalogue record for this book is available from the British Library.

A catalog record for this book is available from the Library of Congress.

10 9 8 7 6 5 4 3 2 1
22 21 20 19 18 17 16 15 14 13

Printed and bound in Great Britain by
CPI Antony Rowe, Chippenham and Eastbourne

Contents

Tables

Figures

Preface

Reflections on developing countries

I am a child of emerging markets, having lived in some of the world's poorest developing countries in Asia, Africa and the Middle East from a relatively early age. Among my recollections from this period is having witnessed famine and abject poverty in Ethiopia. My father would load the back of our Land Rover every weekend with large bags of bread and packets of salt and I would help him to distribute these to those in desperate need whom we saw begging for food on the roadside in the rural areas outside of Addis Ababa. He knew the dangers of salt deficiency in famines in hot climates from having lived through the Bengal famine of 1943.

I cannot adequately describe the wretched condition of the people that we came across during these trips. The closest thing I can compare them to are the haunting photos of the concentration camp prisoners that I saw during a visit to the Bergen-Belsen concentration camp memorial and mass graves of the camp victims while I was staying in northern Germany a few years later. Ironically, when I visited Belsen, I was actually living in a former regimental barracks of the loathsome SS that was being used as one of the bases for the British Army on the Rhine.

Mixed in with these memories of the tragic plight of the rural poor in Ethiopia were exciting memories of adventure. Particularly memorable was the experience of the long drive of over 1,000 kilometres from Addis Ababa to Asmara and back in the trusty Land Rover. It was almost a one-way trip. A hair-raising moment occurred when the front wheel of the Land Rover skidded off the narrow and rough gravel track on the edge of a mountainside, and we gingerly climbed out and unloaded the back of the Land Rover, then pulled it with ropes back onto the road. It was a cameo reminiscent of the final scene from *The Italian Job* with Michael Caine, except that we were playing for real! "Hang on a minute, lads. I've got a great idea!"

This was an unrivalled education in the wild beauty and ruggedness of the East African countryside, where I witnessed the spectacular sight of the Blue Nile Falls, saw early excavations of what was believed to be one of the Queen of Sheba's palaces, hiked in the East African Rift Valley and saw a monstrous giant Nile perch caught in a Rift Valley lake landed by an angler.

Living in Somalia was an even greater adventure, with regular weekend hunting trips in the countryside, which had an abundance of guinea fowl, gazelle, a smaller deer called a dik dik, and warthogs. These trips were no aristocratic pastime, but were necessitated by the shortage of any safe sources of fresh meat in the local markets of Mogadishu, which seemed to lack any supermarkets at all. This was therefore a serious business, as an unsuccessful hunting trip meant a diet of rice, vegetables and fruits for the week ahead.

In contrast with East Africa, India seemed rather sophisticated in terms of living standards. Nevertheless, I recall the difficult conditions in India, where even some of our close relatives, who would have been considered to be in the middle class of India at that time, still had to use wood or coal in their kitchens as their fuel for cooking, and money was certainly scarce. Power blackouts were commonplace in India, whether in the large cities or in regional towns and cities. We spent a significant part of the evenings without electricity, relying on candles. The great upside of this, although we did not perceive it that way at the time, was that it encouraged families and friends to spend long hours socialising or playing board games such as carrom in the candlelight.

When we visited family in various parts of India, it seemed that those relatives who had the least were often the most generous and open-hearted, welcoming us to stay in their homes for long periods of time when we were visiting, and sharing everything they had with us. I remember accompanying my father to the home of a former Sikh driver who had worked for my grandfather. He and his family were thrilled to see us. Their home would probably be considered a slum dwelling by the standards of developed countries, but we spent the most fantastic afternoon with these noble and generous people, and they treated us to a delicious Punjabi meal which I still remember vividly.

My memories of living in Burma are of a country with a great abundance of natural beauty and without the grinding poverty of India or Ethiopia. We often visited the Shwedagon Pagoda in Rangoon at weekends, which must surely be one the greatest cultural treasures in the world.

Poverty and hardship are also relatively recent memories in Northeast Asia. When I lived in Japan, which was already one of the richest countries in the world at that time, I recall an elderly Japanese executive who was very comfortably off telling me about his teenage life in Kobe after the end of the Second World War. The city had been flattened by

US bombing raids. I have seen aerial photos of Kobe at that time, and it had virtually been razed to the ground. He told me how he had to walk in the hillsides around Kobe to search for roots and other edible things from the forests in order to find sufficient food for his family to eat. I heard similar tales of hardship from an old South Korean friend who had been through the Korean War, and he also described times of food shortages and devastation immediately after the end of that war. A young Chinese scholar once related to me the experiences of his parents during the Chinese famine under Mao's rule, and the catastrophic circumstances that befell many rural communities in China, when millions died of starvation.

My own emerging markets experience also included some bitter first-hand tastes of political risk at the sharp end, living through a coup and two wars. I recall moments when there were bullets zipping past my head and when I had to take cover in ditches as fighter jets were strafing and bombing overhead.

War was the crucible in which modern Asia was forged, during the Asia-Pacific conflict in the Second World War. Asia has seen great progress as well as terrible human tragedy since the Second World War. A number of Asian economies have lifted themselves from developing to developed nations within not much more than one generation. The 'Asian Miracle' that occurred in Japan, South Korea, Taiwan and Singapore has created models that other Asian countries now aspire to.

How Singapore's first Prime Minister, Lee Kuan Yew, led his newly independent nation from being a poor developing country to being a highly advanced international business hub and leading financial centre within one generation, eradicating corruption and organised crime along the way, is one of the greatest economic development stories in world history.

The rise of Asian emerging market multinationals has also been spectacular. I relied on a Taiwanese multinational, Acer, for its IT hardware technology when writing this book: a fantastic product. My travels to visit Asian countries are usually with Singapore Airlines, which for over twenty years has been my gold standard for efficient, high-quality air travel. South Korean cars are another icon, with various models of Hyundai cars having been in continuous use by my family for the last two decades, with zero breakdowns on the road in all that time after 300,000 kilometres of Hyundai driving!

The rise of emerging Asian economies in recent decades has resulted in substantial improvements in living standards for hundreds of millions of Asians. If emerging Asia can maintain strong growth over the next thirty years, this has the potential to lift hundreds of millions more out of abject poverty.

Many people have been positive influences on my life and work, and I would also like to acknowledge their help during my many years of work on the Asia-Pacific economies.

I would first like to acknowledge the research help of Danika Biswas for this book, which is much appreciated.

I would also like to particularly thank Zbyszko Tabernacki, Indrajit Coomaraswamy, Paul Morris, Vivek Tulpule, Marc Buedenbender and Brad Holzberger for their encouragement and support for my work, including but not exclusively on Asia-Pacific issues, in various organisations I have worked in during my career. I would also like to thank Tan Sri Dato Michael Yeoh, Yong Ngee Ng, Dr. Frank-Jürgen Richter, Heng Qian and Ambassador Pradap Pibulsonggram for their great helpfulness over the years. I am also most appreciative of the advice and guidance from the editorial team at Palgrave Macmillan, particularly Taiba Batool.

The views and opinions expressed in this book are entirely my own, based on a lifetime of observing the Asia-Pacific region, and should not be attributed in any way to any organisation I have worked for or been associated with, whether public or private, or to any other person.

Special thanks are also due to Matti and Kerstin for inspiration, helping me to climb my own personal 'Nordwand'.

Introduction

The new gold rush in Asia

The new gold rush

In 1848, the discovery of gold at Sutter's Mill in California triggered a gold rush, with an estimated 300,000 persons becoming prospectors in difficult conditions. People came from all corners of the earth to seek their fortune, including from Europe, China, Australia and Latin America. Just three years later, significant gold finds in New South Wales and Victoria in Australia started a new gold rush, which also attracted fortune-hunters from many parts of the world. In the 1880s, another gold rush started in Western Australia, in what were to become the famed goldfields of Kalgoorlie, which remains a major gold mining town to this day.

In the 19th century, those seeking their fortune as gold prospectors faced a very hard and often dangerous life, travelling by mule, horse or even foot to reach the goldfields with their meagre possessions of basic gold mining equipment and essential provisions.

Today, there is a new gold rush taking place in the Asia-Pacific. This time, those seeking their fortune often arrive by commercial jet aircraft, dressed in suits, armed with corporate credit cards and staying in luxury hotels. However, their hunt for gold is much the same as in the 19th century.

The gold they are seeking comes in different forms from the nuggets sought by the prospectors of the past. The new gold takes the form of consumer spending by Asia's fast-growing middle classes, as nations that used to be very poor just three decades ago are becoming middle-income economies. Opportunities abound for firms that can meet the fast-growing consumer demand of the Asia-Pacific for a wide range of products, including automobiles, motorbikes, food products, household goods, information technology products and luxury goods. For aircraft manufacturers, the Asia-Pacific is forecast to be a leading global growth market for decades ahead, as rapidly growing demand for air travel is generating strong commercial aircraft orders. Demand is also rising rapidly for services, such as financial services, tourism and logistics, driven by rising household incomes in many Asian countries.

As the global financial crisis that began in 2008–09 has progressively ravaged Europe and also triggered a recession in the US as well as sharply higher unemployment in many of the developed countries of the OECD, the lure of the Asia-Pacific has increased for those seeking their fortunes. There is a growing flow of workers from the developed countries of the Eurozone, the UK and the US into the Asia-Pacific, as it is seen as the region of fast growth and opportunity for the future. Indeed, the emigration has not been limited to the Asia-Pacific, but also extends to other emerging markets. The disillusion about the future of Europe amongst its citizens is reflected well in the increasing outflow of Portuguese citizens to their former African colony of Mozambique, one of the world's fastest-growing but poorest countries, as Portugal experiences protracted recessionary conditions and high unemployment.

However, it is the Asia-Pacific that remains the magnet for much of the emigration from the developed world. The international cities of Hong Kong and Singapore remain highly competitive business hubs for multinationals, helped by good governance, efficient work practices, low taxation and relatively favourable immigration laws for expatriate workers. These two cities are therefore important hubs for those seeking their fortunes in Asia. However, there are also strong flows of expatriates into the larger industrial economies of Asia, such as mainland China, South Korea, India, Indonesia, Malaysia and Thailand, as these fast-developing economies also generate burgeoning new opportunities in a wide range of industries.

The new frontier economies of Asia, such as Mongolia, Vietnam, Laos, Cambodia, Bangladesh, Sri Lanka and Myanmar, also offer considerable opportunities for investors with a high tolerance for significant risk. These frontier economies remain relatively poor and underdeveloped, but fast economic growth and rapid development are generating new opportunities.

As the world economy faces the challenges of weakening economic growth in Europe and Japan over the next three decades, due to the effects of demographic ageing and ongoing fiscal consolidation to reduce high government debt levels, the rising economic powers of emerging Asia will provide new growth momentum for the global economy.

In the past three decades, the world economy was driven by the US, the EU and Japan, fuelled by the domestic demand of these three economic powers. Over the next three decades, there will be a different set of growth engines for the global economy, notably concentrated in the Asia-Pacific. China, India and the ASEAN economic region will become powerful growth drivers for the world economy, as the combined size of Asian consumer spending becomes an increasingly important engine for global demand growth.

Of course, as former Fed Chairman Alan Greenspan has often stated, 'The business cycle has not been repealed.' China, India and the East Asian region will also face the challenges of the business cycle and external demand shocks from economic events in the US and the EU. Nevertheless, the long-term trends transforming the Asia-Pacific region have been under way for decades, despite major economic shocks such as the East Asian crisis in 1997–98.

By 2025, the shape of the world economy will have changed considerably. China will overtake the US to become the world's largest economy in terms of size of nominal GDP. Similarly, India's GDP will overtake that of Japan by 2025. Indonesia's GDP will exceed two trillion US dollars by 2025, making it one of Asia's largest economies.

However, such seismic shifts in the global economic landscape are also generating competition and conflict. China's rising geopolitical power will be accompanied by significant expansion in the total amount of annual military spending as China's economy becomes the largest in the world. Other Asian countries have watched with alarm as China's rising military capabilities are mixed with outbursts of military posturing against its neighbours, notably over disputed territory in the South China Sea and on the contested Chinese–Indian border. This could increase the risk of an arms race occurring in the Asia-Pacific in the coming decades as countries react to China's military build-up.

A key strategic focus of Chinese policy-makers is on energy security, to ensure that China's fast-growing demand for energy will be adequately met. This is intertwined with the country's foreign policy and defence policy stance, as reflected in China's territorial disputes in the South China Sea, due to potential offshore oil and gas reserves in this area.

Rising Asian demand for energy will also lead to greater competition among the world's largest economies for access to international oil and gas reserves and production, which could escalate tensions between some Asian countries. There may also be increasing political tensions within resource-exporting economies as the large emerging Asian economies, notably China and India, increase their acquisitions of energy assets and other mineral resources in other parts of the world. There have already been cases of such foreign acquisitions of local mineral assets raising political concerns in Australia, Mongolia and Indonesia, and there is a risk of greater resource nationalism as countries seek to protect national ownership of key resources.

The rise of emerging Asian industrial powers is also creating new waves of competition in global industries, as emerging market multinationals compete for market share with multinationals from North America, Europe and Japan. The Japanese semiconductor industry and consumer electronics industry are two high-tech sectors that are already showing significant stress in certain segments due to fierce competition from other Asian countries, notably South Korea.

However, there are also signs of growing political and economic cooperation within Asia in some areas, notably through the success of ASEAN. The ASEAN free trade agreement was implemented at the beginning of 2010, largely removing tariff barriers on trade in goods among the first six ASEAN member countries, with the remainder to follow suit by 2015. The ASEAN+3 Chiang Mai Initiative is another example of regional cooperation in Asian financial markets. ASEAN forums have also been increasingly used as a framework for Asia-Pacific defence talks and confidence-building initiatives to improve regional defence co-operation.

With developed Europe and Japan, two of the world's three main growth engines over the last half century, now facing protracted slow growth, the future of emerging Asia is of critical importance to the long-term global economic outlook. Both developed countries and emerging markets worldwide are increasingly turning their attention to emerging Asia as the new global growth driver for the 21st century.

Chapter 1

From night through blood to light

The Asian ascendancy

...lowliness is young ambition's ladder,
Whereto the climber upward turns his face;
But when he once attains the upmost round,
He then unto the ladder turns his back,
Looks in the clouds, scorning the base degrees
By which he did ascend.

Shakespeare, *Julius Caesar* (2.1.22–27)

'Little Boy' and 'Fat Man'

In August 1945, 'Little Boy' and 'Fat Man' ended the Second World War. When the USAAF B-29 bomber *Enola Gay* dropped the atomic bomb 'Little Boy' on Hiroshima on 6th August, an estimated 69 per cent of the city's buildings were destroyed, with 80,000 persons killed immediately, and another 70,000 persons injured, with most of these wounded to die later from their burns or radiation-related sicknesses. The immediate casualties were around 45 per cent of the total estimated population of Hiroshima.

Despite the scale of this devastation, the Japanese government did not immediately surrender. Three days later, on 9th August, the USAAF B-29 Superfortress *Bockscar* dropped another atomic bomb, 'Fat Man', on Nagasaki, turning the city into rubble. This second atomic bombing forced the Japanese to capitulate, with Emperor Hirohito broadcasting the Japanese surrender on national radio on 15th August.

The formal Japanese surrender was signed aboard the US Navy battleship *USS Missouri* on 2nd September 1945, bringing an end to the Second World War. Although the war was over, much of Asia was in a state of devastation after years of war in the Pacific. A large proportion of the population of Asia had lived in abject poverty even before the beginning of the Second World War, with further deprivation and suffering for large segments of Asia's population during the horrors of the Pacific War. Moreover, much of Asia had been under colonial rule by European powers or Japan at the outset of the Second World War, and the political future was unclear when the war ended.

Japan itself had been totally ravaged by the war its military leaders had started, with the US strategic bombing of Japanese cities having resulted in widespread destruction of 67 major Japanese cities and an estimated 500,000 Japanese deaths. Over half of Tokyo and Kobe had been flattened, with many other Japanese cities having had similar levels of damage inflicted by the USAAF bombing raids. Had Japan not surrendered when it did, more atomic bombs would have been ready for use by September 1945, and Japanese civilian casualties would have been even more catastrophic: indeed, soon after the Nagasaki atomic bombing, a third atom bomb was about to be transported from the US to the Pacific theatre in readiness for use. However, this was not required, as Japan's surrender was announced just in time. It is estimated that altogether around 3.1 million Japanese military and civilians were killed from the time of the Japanese invasion of Manchuria in 1931 until the Japanese surrender in August 1945.

Elsewhere in the Asia-Pacific, there had also been tremendous destruction. After the Soviet Union, China suffered the greatest loss of life during the Second World War. The scale of the horrors inflicted on the Chinese people by the Japanese invasion and occupation that commenced with the Japanese attack on Manchuria is outside the ability of the human mind to comprehend. Estimates of the number of Chinese killed due to war, atrocities and war-related famine during 1937–45 range from 10 to 20 million persons. While the Chinese military had some records of their military casualties, with an estimated 3.2 million Chinese soldiers killed, the scale of civilian loss of life is far more difficult to accurately calculate. The atrocities in just one city indicate the scale of the war crimes inflicted upon the Chinese nation. In relation to the Nanjing massacre committed by the Japanese Army during December 1937, the Nanjing War Crimes Tribunal in 1947 estimated that around 300,000 Chinese civilians and prisoners of war were killed in the atrocities that occurred during the Japanese military occupation.

Much of Southeast Asia also suffered tremendous loss of life as well as destruction of key cities and towns during the Second World War. Burma became a key Pacific battleground, with large-scale military casualties on both sides, first during fierce fighting as the

Japanese pushed the defeated British Army back towards India, and later during the Japanese retreat. After General Slim (later Field Marshal The Viscount Slim) stemmed the tide of Japanese military successes and turned 'Defeat into Victory', thwarting the Japanese advance into northeast India at the battle of Kohima, the Japanese Army suffered tremendous casualties as they retreated back towards Rangoon, pursued by General Slim's British 14th Army, made up of mainly British and Indian troops.

There was also considerable devastation in the Malayan peninsula and Singapore during the Japanese invasion of Malaya in December 1941 and its campaign down the Malayan peninsula to capture Singapore. After the fall of Singapore in February 1942, there were also atrocities committed against the ethnic Chinese population of Singapore, with Japanese troops rounding up thousands of ethnic Chinese civilians and executing them. The total number of persons killed in these executions in Singapore, known as the 'Sook Ching' massacre, is estimated at between 70,000 and 100,000. The end of the fighting in Malaya and Singapore then opened up a new chapter of wartime horrors, as Allied prisoners of war as well as Malay, Indian and Chinese civilian labourers were forced to build a railway between Bangkok and Rangoon in the most appalling conditions, resulting in over 100,000 deaths.

There were an estimated 1 million war-related deaths in the Philippines due to conflict, famine and atrocities. During the final stages of the war, when the Japanese defeat in the Philippines was inevitable, Manila suffered tremendous destruction during the battle between the liberating US forces and the Japanese garrison, with an estimated 100,000 Filipino civilians killed in the city due to bombardment and widespread atrocities by the Japanese troops.

By the time the Second World War had ended, the scale of war-related deaths in the Asia-Pacific theatre due to Japanese territorial ambitions had reached tens of millions. The estimate made by Christopher Bayly and Tim Harper in their excellent book *Forgotten Wars* is that around 30 million persons died as a result of the Pacific War, including around 3 million Indians due to war-related famines.

Merdeka! *The end of European colonialism in Asia*

Such then was the cruel legacy of the Second World War in the Asia-Pacific region. In Asia, as in Europe, the death toll from the war was vast, much of East Asia was left in a state of devastation, and the post-war reconstruction task was immense.

However, the end of the Second World War had also changed global geopolitics fundamentally. The prewar era of European colonialism in Asia that had started in the 16th and 17th centuries with the Dutch East India Company establishing its early settlements in Batavia and Malacca, the Portuguese opening trading posts in Goa and Macau and the British East India Company creating its first trading posts in Surat, Madras, Calcutta and Bombay had finally been shattered by the Second World War. The old European colonial powers had been weakened by the human and financial costs of the war, while Asian nationalist and resistance groups had gained strength during the Allied war against Japan, often helped by Allied military and financial support to fight the Japanese. In some countries the Japanese occupation forces also encouraged some forms of cooperative, local government. Asian nationalism had also been galvanised during the Second World War by the sudden exit of the European colonial rulers. With the rise of Asian nationalist parties in many Asian countries, including Indonesia, India, Burma and Malaya, there was little appetite amongst Asians for reverting to the old times of European colonial rule once the Second World War ended.

This was most forcefully demonstrated in Indonesia, which at the end of the Second World War was still considered by the Allied powers to be a Dutch colony – the Dutch East Indies. As Japan faced the growing inevitability of defeat by 1944, Japanese Prime Minister Koiso made a commitment to eventually permit Indonesian independence. The Japanese occupying forces had allowed the Indonesian nationalist movement to develop under their occupation, albeit in a managed way to assist their own occupation, and this process was advanced more rapidly in the closing months of the Second World War.

The announcement of the Japanese surrender on 15th August 1945 triggered an acceleration of this process to pre-empt the return of the Dutch colonialists, and on 17th August, Indonesian nationalist leaders Sukarno and Mohammed Hatta issued a proclamation of independence with the tacit support of the Japanese occupying forces. With no Dutch colonial administration or military forces present in Indonesia, and the Japanese giving up control of the cities to the new Indonesian republican movement, Indonesian self-government rapidly spread across the major cities. A new Indonesian central government was formed in Jakarta, with

Sukarno elected as President by the Central Indonesian National Committee and plans initiated for general elections to be held.

However, Indonesia's independence was not to be won so easily. When British and Australian troops landed in Indonesia in September 1945 to take over from the Japanese in a caretaker capacity pending the return of the Dutch, the political and military situation rapidly turned into chaos. Dutch administrators and freed Dutch military prisoners of war attempted to re-establish their colonial rule in areas where the Allied forces were in control. During late 1945 and in early 1946, there were fierce battles between the Indonesian republican forces and the Dutch and British as the former attempted to resist efforts by the British Army and Dutch colonial forces to take control of Indonesian cities. Savage fighting took place in various Indonesian cities, including Bandung, Surabaya and Jakarta.

The battle for Surabaya became legendary in Indonesia's struggle for independence. British troops landed in Surabaya on 25th October 1945, and ordered Indonesian revolutionary forces to surrender their weapons. Fearing a return to Dutch rule, the Indonesian forces engaged in a fierce battle. A brief truce proved unsuccessful, and on 10th November fighting commenced again. Three weeks of bitter fighting ensued, which resulted in massive destruction of the city and an estimated 80 per cent of Surabaya's population fleeing. There was substantial loss of life on both sides.

However, despite determined and stubborn resistance, the ill-trained and poorly equipped republican forces were unable to retain control against the strength of the British and Dutch military, and were eventually forced out of the major cities.

As the Dutch military reorganised following the end of the Second World War, the Netherlands sent a strong contingent of their armed forces to reoccupy what they still regarded as their colony. For the next three years, there was a bitter war of independence, as Indonesian revolutionary forces fought the Dutch troops. Although the Dutch succeeded in gaining control of much of urban Indonesia, the revolutionary fires in the hearts of the Indonesian population were no longer going to be extinguished. Ruthless military repression by the Dutch occupying forces attracted growing international criticism, most importantly from the United States. As the Dutch were heavily reliant on US Marshall Aid for the reconstruction of their own war-ravaged country, they were eventually forced by international political pressure to agree to Indonesian independence. On 27th December 1949, Indonesia finally became a sovereign state. On 28th September 1950, Indonesia became the fiftieth member of the United Nations.

Southeast Asia's other independence movements

Elsewhere in Southeast Asia, the retreat of colonialism was also accelerated by the Second World War and the significant weakening of the European colonial powers.

After a long period of British colonial rule that began in 1886, Burma was given independence from Britain in January 1948 in a peaceful transition process, although the nationalist leader Aung San and other key members of his party were assassinated some months before independence, which most likely changed Burma's political and economic destiny for decades to come.

In Malaya, the British and Malay police and military forces fought a long – but ultimately successful – war to suppress a communist insurgency prior to Malaya's independence. However, unlike the Dutch in Indonesia, the British colonial administration worked with Malayan political leaders for a peaceful transition to independence. The first Prime Minister of the Federation of Malaya, Tunku Abdul Rahman, read out the Proclamation of Independence of Malaya from Great Britain at the Merdeka Stadium on 31st August 1957, and he thrilled the new nation as he ended his speech by crying out *Merdeka* ('freedom') seven times. He also set out a vision for the new country to establish an international benchmark for good governance and democracy:

> I call upon you all to dedicate yourselves to the service of the new Malaya: To work and strive with hand and brain to create a new nation, inspired by the ideals of justice and liberty – a beacon of light in a disturbed and distracted world. (Tunku Abdul Rahman, first Prime Minister of the Federation of Malaya, 31st August 1957, Proclamation of Independence speech at Merdeka Stadium)

However, Britain's military involvement in Malaya was not yet over. At the time of Malaya's independence, Malaya and Britain had signed the Anglo-Malayan Defence Agreement, under which Britain provided guarantees to defend the independence of Malaya. This agreement was put to intensive use over the next decade to thwart Indonesian aggression.

Indonesia became increasingly threatening in its stance towards plans laid out in 1961 for the creation of Malaysia through the integration of the British colonies of North Borneo, Sarawak, Singapore and Brunei. An Indonesian-backed coup attempt in Brunei in December 1962 was thwarted by the deployment of British Army Gurkha troops. The Indonesian position escalated further in 1963 when Sukarno decided to pursue a policy of 'Konfrontasi' with the newly created Malaysia, resulting in extensive joint Malaysian and British military operations on the Indonesian border to prevent Indonesian military incursions, with many border clashes as Commonwealth forces defended the Malaysian border regions.

An Indonesian parachute drop of a small detachment of paramilitary forces into Johor in Malaya in 1964 proved to be a debacle, but it escalated tensions between Indonesia and Britain to the brink of full-scale military conflict. The UK sent a carrier task force into regional waters, sailing through the Indonesian archipelago, and it took considerable behind-the-scenes US diplomacy with both the UK and Indonesia to prevent an escalating conflict with aggressive British counter-strikes. The US was already engaged in military conflicts in Vietnam and Laos, and was anxious to avoid Southeast Asia's most populous country turning into a third theatre of war in the region.

According to CIA estimates at the time, there were 400–500 Indonesian forces on the Malaysia–Borneo border ready to enter Malaysian territory on special operations, with around 1,600 Indonesian guerrillas committed to the 'Konfrontasi' campaign (sourced from Memorandum from McCafferty to McGeorge Bundy, the US President's Special Assistant for National Security Affairs, 11th March 1965, Johnson Library, National Security File, Country File Indonesia, Vol. IV, Memos, 3/65–9/65).

In a secret conversation between Indonesian Defence Minister General Nasution and US Ambassador Howard Jones, which took place in the US Embassy in Jakarta in 1964, General Nasution stated that the Indonesian armed forces were strongly pro-US and anti-communist, and that the policy of 'Konfrontasi' was a direct result of Sukarno's efforts to maintain his popular support and deflect popular attention away from the economic crisis and hardships the Indonesian population was experiencing.

The period of 'Konfrontasi' only ended after Major General Suharto ousted Sukarno from power, after Suharto had led the armed forces in thwarting a communist coup plot by the Partai Kommunis Indonesia (PKI). Although Britain's defence guarantee under the bilateral defence agreement with Malaysia ended in 1967, a successor Five Power Defence Agreement between Britain, Malaysia, Singapore, Australia and New Zealand was signed in 1971, which remains in place at the present time.

The rise of communism in Asia

Indonesia's PKI and the 1965 coup attempt

The PKI's membership had been growing very rapidly during the period between 1961 and 1965, with President Sukarno giving the PKI increasing influence within his party and key government institutions in order to maintain power, yet attempting to play a game of brinkmanship to appease the armed forces and Muslim parties, whose support he also needed. The rising influence of the PKI was reflected in a cabinet reshuffle in August 1964 which resulted in the appointment of three PKI members as ministers, as well as three PKI sympathisers to ministerial posts. By late 1964 the rise of the PKI was creating a significant likelihood that the communists could eventually win a power struggle after the age-ing Sukarno's death.

However, the PKI did not wait for such a political succession, and instead forced events to a head with a coup attempt on 30th September 1965. Led by some senior military officers in Jakarta, including Lieutenant Colonel Untung, the commander of the Tjakrabirawa battalion of presidential guards, the coupists seized key Indonesian military leaders and brutally murdered them as part of efforts to assume control of the government. Nasution was on the list of army generals whom the coup plotters had attempted to capture, but he had managed to escape from his home as the coupists entered. Nasution had already once put down a rebellion by pro-communist soldiers in Madiun, and for the coupists, this was a dangerous foe that they had let slip through their fingers.

Within hours the coup attempt quickly faltered, as General Nasution led armed forces in seizing back control of key installa-tions in Jakarta, supported by General Suharto, a young military leader who had risen to prominence during the war of independ-ence against the Dutch, and who was now commander of the Army Strategic Reserve (KOSTRAD).

With the Army Commander General Yani having been mur-dered in the coup, General Suharto assumed command of the army. President Sukarno himself was considered to have prior knowledge of the coup plot, and was isolated by Suharto's troops surrounding his palace, with Suharto and other military leaders essentially taking control of government.

The PKI had given the Indonesian armed forces the opportunity they had wanted to crush communism in Indonesia. Nasution's own five-year-old daughter had been murdered by the coupists during the firefight when they stormed his house, fuelling his own determination to crush the communists. The brutal execution of the Indonesian generals by the coupists would undoubtedly also have enraged the majority of the armed forces.

In the following months, Nasution and Suharto led the armed forces in a ruthless purge of communist party members throughout Indonesia, supported by Muslim groups and pro-military youth movements. The estimated total deaths during the purge range from 200,000 up to 1 million, with a great deal of uncertainty about the exact number of killings due to the state of anarchy and chaos that prevailed, with many non-communists also being killed in the confusion as opportunists settled old scores.

> Moslem fervor in Atjeh apparently put all but a few PKI out of action. Atjehnese have decapitated PKI and placed their heads on stakes along the road. (Telegram 1269 from US Embassy in Jakarta to US State Department, 29th October 1965 (in *Foreign Relations of the United States, 1964–68*, Vol. XXVI, page 338, 'Indonesia, Malaysia-Singapore, Philippines', US National Security Archive))

Six months after the coup, a secret US Embassy assessment – which was later declassified under US government freedom of information rules – gives an indication of the great uncertainty regarding the death toll due to the purge of the PKI:

> We frankly do not know whether the real figure is 100,000 or 1,000,000 but believe it is wiser to err on the side of the lower estimates, especially when questioned by the press. (Declassified communication from US Embassy, Jakarta to US State Department, 15th April 1966 (in *Foreign Relations of the United States, 1964–68*, Vol. XXVI, page 339, 'Indonesia, Malaysia-Singapore, Philippines', US National Security Archive))

However, an earlier US Embassy communication in February 1966 estimated the death toll in Bali alone at over 80,000, indicating that the scale of the purge was most likely to have been significantly higher than the lower bound of these estimates.

Although the rising tide of communism in Indonesia was crushed in 1965 by the Indonesian armed forces, elsewhere in Asia communist movements had managed to seize power, most notably in China, North Vietnam and North Korea.

Vietnam: the road to Dien Bien Phu

The Second World War was the catalyst for the end of French colonial rule in Indochina, although, like the Dutch in Indonesia, the French fought to keep their foothold in Vietnam. Vietnam had been gradually colonised by the French in the late 19th century, after French military attacks on Danang in 1858 and Saigon in 1859 to protect Catholic missionaries from persecution. France gradually built up its territorial possessions in southern Vietnam. In 1864, the French government formally made the territorial acquisitions in southern Vietnam, known as Cochinchina, into a French territory. By 1887, France had also acquired northern Vietnam from China after winning the Sino-French War of 1884–85. Cambodia had also become a French protectorate after this was requested by the Cambodian king. Therefore by 1887, France had established French Indochina, which would remain a French colony until the Second World War.

With the defeat of France by the invading Nazi forces in 1940, the Vichy government came to power in France as a puppet government established by the Germans. French Indochina came under Vichy administration, and although Indochina remained under French rule, it was required to sign an agreement that allowed limited Axis forces to be based in Indochina. As soon as the agreement was signed, Japanese troops entered Indochina in strength. This actually triggered a battle between French troops and Japanese forces, as the French administration feared the Japanese would simply take control of Indochina. After negotiations between the French Vichy government and the Japanese government, the Japanese army ceased its attacks. An uneasy co-existence commenced, with Japanese forces occupying key military airfields and port facilities essential for their strategic plans for conquest of the Asia-Pacific. In July 1941, the agreement between the Vichy government and Japan was strengthened further, in effect allowing Japanese forces complete access to Indochina, and Japan also signed an agreement whereby it would have almost exclusive rights to the agricultural and mineral exports of Vietnam.

This economic agreement became the cause of considerable suffering for the Vietnamese people, as Japan exploited Vietnamese resources for its own war efforts. With its food production being drained by the Japanese, Vietnam experienced a severe famine in 1944–45 as a result of the combined effects of a drought in northern Vietnam and rice being taken for the use of the Japanese army. The total number of deaths as a result of the famine has been estimated as ranging between 400,000 and 2 million people. French colonial administration estimates at the time ranged from 400,000 to 1 million, while the Vietnamese communist forces put the estimate as high as 2 million people.

In any case, the famine represented a tragedy for the Vietnamese people, and became an important source of rising nationalist sentiment and support for the Vietnamese communist guerrillas. This provided considerable momentum for the Vietnamese communist movement, the Viet Minh, led by Ho Chi Minh. The US and British military provided support for the Viet Minh in their fight against the Japanese, with the US Office of Strategic Services, the forerunner of the CIA, involved in this military co-operation.

Following the atomic bombings of Japan in August 1945, the Japanese forces in Vietnam chose to surrender to the local nationalist forces of the Viet Minh rather than to the French colonial forces, and this provided the moment of opportunity that Ho Chi Minh had awaited. Having acquired considerable Japanese military equipment from the Japanese army, Ho Chi Minh proclaimed the independence of Vietnam on 2nd September 1945.

What followed was very similar to the pattern of events in Indonesia. British units from the 14th Army together with French troops re-occupied Saigon in late September, which led to bitter fighting between French troops and the Viet Minh in Hai Phong and Saigon by 1946. The Viet Minh were pushed out of the cities, as had occurred with the Indonesian republican forces in their war with the Dutch colonial forces, but ongoing insurgency intensified as the Viet Minh pursued an effective guerrilla campaign.

The turning point for the Viet Minh came when the Chinese communists took power in China in 1949, providing the Viet Minh with strong support across their border with northern

Vietnam. The Viet Minh campaign culminated in a major victory against the French forces at Dien Bien Phu in 1954, forcing the French to concede an agreement at the Geneva Conference of 1954 for the partition of Vietnam, with the creation of communist North Vietnam. Although southern Vietnam remained under the control of a pro-French government, the die was cast for the next phase of the war in Vietnam, in which southern Vietnamese forces with US support would be engaged in a bitter war against North Vietnamese communist forces committed to unification of Vietnam. This would culminate in a communist victory and the unification of Vietnam in 1975, and would bring devastation to Laos and Cambodia in the process.

The rise of communism in Northeast Asia

In China, communist forces led by Mao Zedong had succeeded in ousting the Chinese Nationalist Government under Chiang Kai-shek, forcing it to flee into exile on the island of Formosa (Taiwan). Over the next five years, between 1 and 2 million persons were killed as the communists attempted to purge Chinese society of Nationalist Party supporters as well as people they identified as capitalists, such as landowners, businessmen and persons with ties to foreign businesses. Chairman Mao himself said that 700,000 persons were executed during this period, although hundreds of thousands probably perished in the labour camps where those who were identified as capitalist elements were sent, ostensibly for reform.

The fate of Korea was to be similar to that of Vietnam, with the nation politically split after the end of colonial rule. Japan's occupation of Korea occurred as a result of Japan's victory in the Russo-Japanese War of 1905. In the post-war treaty between Russia and Japan signed in September 1905, Russia agreed to Japan's claims to Korea. Formal annexation of Korea by Japanese forces took place in 1910, and Japanese occupation forces ruled Korea until 1945. At the end of the Second World War, under a United Nations Agreement for the administration of the Korean peninsula after the defeat of Japan, it was agreed that the Soviet Union would administer the Korean peninsula above the 38th Parallel while the US would administer the southern part. The puppet communist government installed by the Soviet Union in the north officially became an independent nation in 1948, led by

Kim Il-sung. Meanwhile, South Korea had also become an independent state after general elections were held in 1948.

The decision by the US to withdraw most of its troops from South Korea created the opportunity the North was waiting for in its quest to create a unified communist Korea, and North Korea invaded the South in June 1950, prompting US and United Nations military intervention to save South Korea. The US-led counterattack, built on General MacArthur's daring amphibious landings at Incheon, allowed US forces to quickly retake Seoul and cut off the North Korean supply lines, forcing North Korean forces to rapidly retreat towards the North Korean border with China. MacArthur's counterattack was so successful that it began to threaten the Pyongyang regime's survival. This prompted China to enter the war to prevent the creation of a US-supported unified Korea on China's flank. An estimated 2 million persons died in the Korean War, which continued until July 1953.

China's famine

Asia's human tragedies since the beginning of the Second World War had been devastating, but perhaps the worst human disaster of all to befall Asia in the 20th century was the direct result not of war, but of fatally flawed communist economic policies. As in the Soviet Union, the great famine that took place in China under communist rule was largely self-inflicted, due to the impact of Stalinist policies of rural collectivisation that were an utter failure. The collectivisation of rural China into 26,000 communes during Mao's 'Great Leap Forward', together with government policies that forced farmers out of their farming collectives to work on industrial and irrigation projects, resulted in a collapse of farm output by 1958.

The Soviet Union had experienced devastating famines under Stalin's collectivisation policies in the 1930s. However, China's famine during the period 1958–62 wrought even more catastrophic consequences on its population, resulting in an estimated death toll that ranges from 35 to 50 million persons, with some of the most in-depth analyses by modern Chinese historians indicating a figure of around 40 million deaths due to this famine, and some Chinese expert estimates ranging from 46 million to 55 million. Whether the true figure was 40 million or as high as 55 million will never be known, but even at the lower end of the range, this far exceeds the estimated death toll in China due to the Japanese occupation in the Second World War, which was already an extreme catastrophe in the annals of world history.

Indian independence

While British armed forces were attempting to protect the colonial interests of the Dutch in Indonesia and the French in Vietnam, British colonialism in Asia was itself in retreat. The Indian nationalist movement that had grown in strength during the Second World War, mainly through the non-violent freedom movements led by Mahatma Gandhi and Jawaharlal Nehru, culminated with the British granting independence to India on 15th August 1947, exactly two years after the Japanese surrender that ended the Second World War.

The speed with which British rule in India ended after two centuries of colonisation reflected both the widespread support within India for the freedom movement and the recognition by the British government that Britain, weakened by the Second World War, was unwilling and unable to pour sufficient resources into the Indian subcontinent to preserve its colonial rule. Lord Louis Mountbatten, appointed by British Labour Prime Minister Clement Attlee to oversee the transition to Indian independence, was also a highly intelligent and pragmatic leader who understood and was sympathetic to the aspirations of the Asian colonies of European powers for self-rule. However, despite the peaceful protest movement in India led by Gandhi, India's freedom was also born in blood. Following extremely difficult negotiations with Jinnah, leader of the Muslim League, the British decided that the terms of independence required the partition of India into two separate nations, India and Pakistan.

The physical division of what had been British India into different sovereign nations based on religion resulted in one of the bloodiest episodes in the annals of Asian history. Partition triggered widespread communal violence, with estimates of the death toll ranging between half a million and 1 million persons. In the state of anarchy and chaos that ruled in the regions affected, there are no definitive records of how many souls perished. After Gandhi had made India famous and respected internationally for the success of its non-violent protests, India now descended into an orgy of violence, with many incidents of very gruesome massacres.

Massive movements of refugees took place as violence forced Hindus and Sikhs who lived in areas that had been carved out as the new Pakistan to flee to the safety of India, while millions of Muslims headed in the opposite direction for the territories of the new East and West Pakistan. Estimated flows of displaced persons range around 10–12 million refugees due to the partition.

The partition of India traumatised a generation of Indians and Pakistanis who lived through these times. My mother's family and many of their relatives were among the refugees who lost everything as they fled from Lahore, which was in the new state of Pakistan, to resettle in various parts of northern India. My father, from Bengal, another part of the country that was badly affected by partition, would only ever hint at the horrors he witnessed as a teenager living through some of the communal massacres. He was never willing to describe the full details of what he had witnessed as the details were evidently too terrible to recount to his children.

However, there are many testimonies and accounts of the violence that took place. In Alex von Tunzelmann's book *Indian Summer: The Secret History of the End of an Empire*, there are detailed descriptions of some of the communal violence that took place, with an estimated 15,000–20,000 deaths and serious injuries in Calcutta.

> On the morning of 16th August, Calcutta erupted into a frenzy of violence. Groups of Muslims, Hindus and the small community of Sikhs attacked each other in the streets. Others formed murder squads to venture into different quarters of the town, killing, beating and raping anyone they could find. Their sadism knew no bounds. (*Indian Summer*, Alex von Tunzelmann, Part One, "Empire", page 143, Pocket Books, 2008)

The deep hatred generated by partition between large segments of the populations in India and Pakistan also created territorial disputes over divided Kashmir, which sewed the seeds for decades of military confrontation that continue until this day. India and Pakistan have also fought several wars, including the 1947–48 Kashmir War, the 1965 War and the 1971 War, with other major border clashes such as the Kargil Conflict in 1999, which brought both nations to the brink of all-out war.

The beginning of Asia's economic ascent

The Asia-Pacific at the end of the Second World War was an extremely poor, underdeveloped region of the world economy. Whereas the US had developed the Marshall Aid programme for the reconstruction of post-war Europe, there was no equivalent programme for Asia.

China and India, the two most populous nations of the globe, had incomes per capita that were amongst the lowest in the world, with still predominantly agrarian subsistence economies and the bulk of their populations living in extreme poverty. Japan after the Second World War was a nation that had been destroyed by the war, with its major cities in ruins. South Korea after the Korean War was also a nation in extreme poverty, after decades of colonial rule by Japan and ravaged by the war with North Korea.

The per capita GDP of South Korea in 1955 was estimated at around 9 per cent of that of the US, only slightly better than that of India, which was estimated to be just 6.5 per cent of US per capita GDP. Chinese GDP per capita was similar to that of India. Indonesia was poorer still, with per capita GDP at around 6 per cent of the US figure in 1955. Even Japan, which had been an industrialised economy before the Second World War, had seen its relative per capita GDP decline to just 27 per cent of that of the US by 1955. Asia was essentially mired in poverty with little prospect of significant change foreseeable.

Table 1.1 GDP per capita, Asian countries compared with leading Western nations (measured in constant prices, 1990 international dollars)

	1900	1913	1950	1973	1992
Asia region	775	872	863	2,442	5,294
China	652	688	614	1,186	3,098
India	625	663	597	853	1,348
Indonesia	745	917	874	1,538	2,749
Japan	1,135	1,334	1,873	11,017	19,425
South Korea	850	948	876	2,840	10,010
Taiwan	759	794	922	3,669	11,590
Thailand	812	846	848	1,750	4,694
Western countries					
US	4,096	5,307	9,573	16,607	21,558
UK	4,593	5,032	6,847	11,992	15,738
Germany	3,134	3,833	4,281	13,152	19,351
France	2,849	3,452	5,221	12,940	17,959

Source: 'Monitoring the World Economy 1820–1992', Angus Maddison, Development Centre Studies, OECD, 1995.

However, this was the beginning of Asia's remarkable economic ascent over the next six decades. Japan's economy was galvanised by the Korean War and the US demand for Japanese products to support its military presence in Asia. The strong growth of both the US and Western European consumer markets during the 1960s provided a key catalyst for the Asian export growth engine, as a number of East Asian economies embraced an export growth model, with varying degrees of support from government industrial policy initiatives.

The first batch of East Asian tigers that rode the export growth wave during the 1960s comprised Singapore, Hong Kong, Malaysia, Taiwan and South Korea. The rapid growth of their export economies supported by large inward investment inflows by Western multinationals seeking to tap low-cost labour for manufacturing production brought rapid economic development and strong growth in household incomes in these economies.

In contrast, the Asian economies that pursued communist and socialist economic development models remained backward and relatively slow-growing. The populations of Asia's most populous developing countries – China, India and Indonesia – remained mired in extreme poverty, with limited progress in human development indicators between the 1950s and 1970s.

The crucial change that accelerated the economic development of the Asia-Pacific region was the change of economic policy by China in 1978, under the leadership of Senior Leader Deng Xiaoping. Deng's 'Second Revolution' resulted in progressive and crucial liberalisation measures, including a shift away from collective agriculture, which had brought devastating consequences to the Chinese population, as well as the establishment of special economic zones in China's coastal provinces to encourage the growth of export industries. The results of this gradual liberalisation process created an economic miracle in China over the next three decades.

China's achievements in poverty alleviation since 1978 are internationally recognised. The country has significantly reduced the total number of impoverished people, from 250 million people in 1978 to 26.88 million in 2010, and China is the first developing country to meet the United Nations Development Programme Millennium Development Goal of halving its population living in poverty. (Howard Liu Hungto, China Programme Unit Director, Oxfam Hong Kong Press Release, 6th December 2011)

Compared with the Communist Party in China, India's democratically elected governments were laggards in adopting the path of economic liberalisation, clinging to socialist economic development models that emphasised protectionist policies until 1991. Even then, India only shifted its economic path due to a balance of payments crisis during 1990–91 which forced India to negotiate a bailout from the IMF. The collapse of the Chandra Sekhar government in 1991 resulted in Narasimha Rao becoming the Indian Prime Minister, with the able economist Manmohan Singh appointed as Finance Minister. It is Manmohan Singh who initially led India along the path of economic liberalisation, albeit gradually, further catalysed by IMF requirements for economic reforms as part of the conditions for its bailout package.

With China having engineered a breakneck speed of economic growth that averaged 10 per cent real GDP growth per year in the three decades since its economic liberalisation commenced, the size of the Chinese economy as a share of the global economy has become increasingly significant.

During the last decade, India's average economic growth rate has also shifted upwards, with annual GDP growth in the range of 7 to 9 per cent per year, compared with 5 to 6 per cent during the previous three decades.

As a result of these far-reaching changes in Asian economic development, what is the state of Asian economic progress?

In East Asia, the progress in human development indicators has been quite spectacular. Recent World Bank estimates of global poverty levels have calculated that the number of persons living in extreme poverty in East Asia has declined from 77 per cent of the population in 1981 to around 14 per cent of the population in 2008. In South Asia, there has also been significant progress in poverty reduction, albeit the share of the population living in extreme poverty is still high, having declined from 61 per cent in 1981 to an estimated 36 per cent of the population in 2008.

If we use a relative benchmark of per capita GDP compared with the USA, there has been tremendous convergence by a number of East Asian countries. Foremost among these are Singapore and Japan. Singapore did not exist as a sovereign nation in 1955, but its per capita GDP would have been broadly comparable to that of Malaya, which had a per capita GDP of around 13 per cent that of the US. By 2010, Singapore's GDP per capita had reached 92 per cent that of the US, reflecting almost full convergence within 55 years. Japan's per capita GDP is similar, at 91 per cent of US GDP per head. This also represents almost full convergence within less than six decades.

South Korea, which had been one of the world's poorest countries in 1955, has also made huge strides in economic development, with per capita GDP averaging 44 per cent of that of the US by 2010, representing very significant convergence since 1955.

China's convergence seems less impressive at first glance, having reached only 9.4 per cent of US per capita GDP levels by 2010, but given the size of the Chinese population this still represents significant human development. It should also be noted that in 2011, Chinese GDP per capita converged further with the US due to the combined impact of relatively rapid GDP growth of 9 per cent together with currency appreciation of around 6 per cent against the dollar. Therefore in just one year, the Chinese per capita GDP level relative to the US moved to 11.3 per cent of US per capita GDP. Moreover, as will be discussed in Chapter 2 on the long-term outlook, China's economic development is still progressing rapidly, with considerable further progress expected in coming decades.

However, the progress of Asia's other BRIC nations looks considerably less spectacular than China's. With Indian per capita GDP still only around USD 1,400 per capita, India has fallen further behind the US in terms of per capita GDP than in 1955, at only 3 per cent of US GDP per head in 2010, compared with 6.5 per cent in 1955.

Other Asian countries are also experiencing various economic challenges, with Japan now facing tremendous economic problems following the bursting of the Japanese asset bubble in the 1990s,

Table 1.2 Asian per capita GDP compared with the US

USD per person	2010
USA	46,860
Singapore	43,117
Japan	42,783
Hong Kong	31,514
South Korea	20,756
Taiwan	18,558
Malaysia	8,423
China	4,382
Indonesia	2,974
India	1,371

Source: IMF.

a mounting sovereign debt burden and the negative macroeconomic consequences of demographic ageing. China is also facing demographic ageing over the coming decades, which could significantly dampen its economic growth rate.

Meanwhile, many of the East Asian tigers are facing challenges to their traditional competitiveness in manufacturing as a consequence of their own economic success, as rising wage levels erode competitiveness in the low-cost manufacturing industries that were the engines of economic growth in past decades.

Therefore, one of the greatest challenges facing the Asia-Pacific and global economies is whether the Asian economic miracle will continue in the coming decades, or whether Asia's economic ascendancy could face an imminent denouement.

Chapter 2

The new gold rush

The rise of Asian consumer power

Europe's 21st century will be shaped by emerging market economies, of which China's economy will be by far the most important. For the EU, China is already a key trade partner, ranking second only to the US. China and the EU are strategic partners, with EU-China summits which allow for a regular exchange of views. Our positions converge on a significant number of issues.

Jean-Claude Juncker, Prime Minister of Luxembourg, November 2010, speech at Horasis Global China Business Meeting, Luxembourg

The Chairman wears Zegna

A Chinese friend of mine – who is a Beijing-based investment banker – told me he was shopping in New York recently, looking for watches at an up-market department store. The salesperson was showing him the watches. As he was trying them on, he noticed that a shabby-looking Chinese gentleman alongside him who was unable to speak English was not getting any service. My friend asked the saleslady if she wouldn't mind serving his countryman for a moment. She reluctantly agreed, but was unwilling to let the poorly dressed customer handle the watches. Eventually my friend persuaded her to let the Chinese customer try on the watches. After trying on several, he said in Chinese that he wanted to buy three, which my friend translated to the saleslady. The Chinese gentleman opened up his battered briefcase and pulled out thousands of dollars in cash to pay for them. In the best traditions of New York commerce, the saleslady ditched my friend and gave the Chinese gentleman her undivided attention as she processed his transactions, leaving my friend struggling to get served.

Watches play a central role in another anecdote about the spending power of the Chinese consumer. I was part of some negotiations between senior executives of a Chinese investment bank and a Swiss firm in Zürich. After the deal was successfully concluded in the late afternoon, the senior executive leading the Chinese bank's negotiating team said that he now wanted to buy a certain luxury brand Swiss watch. He gave the specifications, and after some frantic telephone calls to some of the famous stores in the Bahnhofstrasse, a shop was identified that had the watch. Switzerland hardly has the same shopping hours as Hong Kong or Singapore, so as it was already 4.30 pm we rushed with the Chinese delegates to the store. Within fifteen minutes, the Chinese executive had decided to buy the watch, which cost a mere 15,000 Swiss Francs (around ten thousand pounds in UK sterling). At this point his number two decided he should follow the example set by his boss, and he bought a watch of the same brand at a similar price, but just a bit cheaper, perhaps so that he would not offend his boss by wearing the exact same model as him. Soon after 5 pm we left the store, with the Chinese executives very pleased with their purchases, and the Swiss saleslady even more thrilled.

The shift from West to East

The world economy is currently going through a major structural transformation due to the sustained rapid economic growth of the Asia-Pacific region. This trend is not new – it began in the 1960s with the rise of Japan as Asia's first industrialised nation, followed by the rapid economic development of other Asian developing economies, including South Korea, Taiwan, Hong Kong and Singapore.

At the outset of the 21st century, there is an even more far-reaching shift in global economic power taking place, due to the rapid economic ascent of China and India. China has already become the world's second largest economy in terms of the total size of its economy, measured in terms of nominal gross domestic droduct (GDP). An even more fundamental change in the economic balance between the Western economies of the US and Europe and the Asia-Pacific economies is about to take place, as China will become the world's largest economy by around 2025, overtaking the US, if it can maintain average real economic growth rates of 7 to 8 per cent per year. The Indian economy is also projected to grow rapidly over the next decade, with India's nominal GDP projected to exceed that of Japan by 2025 based on average real economic growth rates of 7 to 8 per cent per year.

Table 2.1 Distribution of world GDP, 1820–1992

	1820	**1992**
Asia	405	10,287
Europe	229	8,282
US, Canada, ANZ	14	6,359
Latin America	14	2,225
Africa	33	842
World	695	27,995

Source: 'Monitoring the World Economy 1820–1992', Angus Maddison, Development Centre Studies, OECD, 1995.

The implication of the rising relative size of China and India compared with the current leading industrial economies of North America and Western Europe is that there will be a significant shift in global economic power from West to East. While this represents a substantial change in the global economic order within the time frame of the last century, during the era of Western industrialisation as well as colonialism, it represents a shift back to the historical balance prior to the Industrial Revolution, when China and India accounted for a much larger share of the global economy.

Estimates of global GDP distribution undertaken by the distinguished economist Angus Maddison for the OECD have calculated that in 1820, China and India together accounted for 44.7 per cent of global GDP, with Japan accounting for a further 3.1 per cent of world GDP. The Asian region as a whole accounted for 57 per cent of world GDP and 69 per cent of the world population in 1820, according to the OECD estimates.

However, by 1992, China and India together accounted for only 17.1 per cent of world GDP, a very substantial decline compared with 1820. Due to the rapid economic development of Japan after the Second World War, Japan's share of world GDP had risen to 8.6 per cent, which helped to mitigate the overall decline of Asia's share of world GDP. Nevertheless, Asian GDP had declined from 57 per cent of world GDP in 1820 to only 37 per cent of world GDP by 1992.

The rise of Asian economic power

One of the key structural economic trends that will occur due to the fast economic growth of the Asia-Pacific developing countries is the rapid growth in household incomes of ordinary households in many Asian countries. The spending power of middle-class consumers in Asia is forecast to rise dramatically over the next twenty years, making Asian consumer spending an increasingly important driver for global economic growth as well as a far more significant market for international businesses seeking to tap global export opportunities.

According to forecasts by the OECD (OECD Development Centre Working Paper 285, 'The Emerging Middle Class in Developing Countries', by Homi Kharas, January 2010), the Asian consumer will dominate the global growth in middle-class spending power over the next twenty years. The OECD projects that the size of the middle-class population of consumers with spending power of between 10 US dollars and 100 US dollars per day in equivalent purchasing power terms across countries will rise from 1.8 billion people in 2009 to 3.2 billion by 2020 and 4.9 billion by 2030, with 85 per cent of this increase being from Asia.

The implication of the very large rise in the total number of Asian households entering the middle classes over the next twenty years is that Asian consumer markets will be the fastest-growing markets in the world over the next two decades. This will be driven by the rapid growth of consumer spending in fast-growing Asian countries with large populations, notably China, India, Indonesia and Vietnam. When compared with the mature developed markets of Europe and the US, the annual rate of growth of Asian consumer markets will be considerably faster.

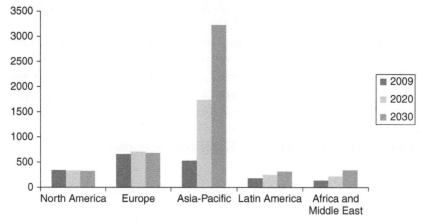

Figure 2.1   The rise of Asian consumer power: total size of consumer middle class to 2030, millions of persons

Source: OECD Development Centre, Working Paper 285, by Homi Karas.

The outlook to 2030

With the number of Asian middle-class consumers set to rise from around 500 million in 2010 to over 3 billion by 2030, Asia's share of the total number of middle-class consumers worldwide will rise from 28 per cent currently to 66 per cent by 2030. This means that the Asian region is on the threshold of becoming the world's most important consumer market.

Such a far-reaching transformation of global consumer markets will underpin a number of strategic shifts in global business:

- The Asia-Pacific region will be the fastest-growing consumer market in the world over the next two decades, whereas retail sales in the European Union will stagnate as a result of protracted weak growth as well as the impact of demographic ageing.
- The rapidly growing size of consumer expenditure in Asia projected over the next twenty years will increasingly result in a major transformation of the structure of global multinational corporations, as US and European multinationals dramatically transform their corporate strategies towards the Asia-Pacific. Asia will account for a higher share of total annual investment, a rising share of total employment and a greater voice in global top management for most multinationals.
- The fast pace of growth in Asian consumer markets will also support the rise of Asian multinationals in many different industry segments, ranging from manufacturing such as automobiles and electronics to services such as banking, insurance and health care.
- The tastes, fashions and preferences of Asian consumers will play an increasingly important role in driving global consumer market trends. The ranks of Generation Y young middle classes in Asia are large and growing, creating considerable purchasing power for luxury products such as watches and designer clothing, as well as for services such as tourism, financial products and health care. With their strong focus on IT connectivity through mobile phones and laptops, they are also changing the world of advertising increasingly towards digital media.

Most important of all, the strong pace of expansion of Asian consumer demand will be an increasingly significant growth driver for the world economy, providing a strong underpinning for sustained rapid growth in world trade.

The age of the Chinese consumer

Since the sustained liberalisation of the Chinese economy commenced in 1978, exports and investment have been the main
growth engines of the Chinese economic miracle, driving a far-
reaching transformation of the Chinese economy. In contrast,
household consumption as a share of GDP has gradually declined,
and is currently estimated to account for around 33 per cent of
GDP, compared with around 55 per cent of GDP in the early 1980s.
This is very low in comparison with most other large developed
and developing economies, and has made China too dependent
on export- and investment-led growth.

However, there is a major rebalancing taking place in the structure of the Chinese economy, which, over the next decade, is
expected to result in a significant shift away from the traditional
growth engines of exports and investment, towards domestic
demand-driven growth. This reflects a number of factors.

First, rapid growth in wages is expected to support strong
medium-term expansion in consumer demand, helping to boost
the share of consumption in GDP over the long term. Large annual
increases in minimum wages across Chinese provinces, together
with double-digit growth in manufacturing wages, particularly
in the Pearl River delta and Yangtze River delta, are helping to
underpin consumer spending. Chinese manufacturing wages will
continue to show strong annual growth over the medium term,
supporting rising household incomes and driving consumer
spending.

Secondly, the nature of Chinese household consumption has
transformed significantly over the last two decades, as Chinese
economic development has resulted in rapid growth in average
GDP per person. In 1978, at the beginning of the economic liberalisation process, nominal GDP per person in US dollars was
estimated to be USD 225. Decades of sustained rapid growth have
resulted in a far-reaching reduction in poverty levels as well as
large rises in average GDP per capita, which is forecast to exceed
USD 6,000 in 2012.

The historical experience of other large economies such as the
US and Japan shows that in the early phases of rising incomes,
private consumption as a share of GDP does decline rapidly,
as households shift away from subsistence living standards and
increase their savings rates. However, this process stabilises

relatively quickly, and Chinese GDP per person is now reaching levels at which private consumption should first stabilise as a share of GDP, then gradually move higher. The development of pensions and healthcare systems will also help this process, reducing the need for households to accumulate precautionary savings to cover retirement and health needs.

Thirdly, China's '12th Five Year Plan' also contains key policy elements that will support domestic demand. In particular, the continued strong policy focus on the economic development of China's inland provinces will help to support private consumption growth amongst a large share of China's total population, with an estimated 700 million persons living in the inland provinces. The accelerated economic development of these provinces through large-scale infrastructure and urban development programmes, helped by the relocation of manufacturing inland to benefit from lower wage costs, has boosted consumer spending in much of inland rural China, with rural retail sales up 17.2 per cent year on year in November 2011.

An important new element that the '12th Five Year Plan' introduces is a Domestic Trade Development Plan, which will aim to accelerate the growth of domestic consumption through structural reforms and new consumer incentives, with a key objective to double total retail sales between 2010 and 2015, to reach a level of 30 trillion yuan (USD 4.8 trillion). Key priority segments will be the automotive and retail electrical goods sectors, with home furnishings also a priority given the government has targeted to build 36 million affordable housing units over the duration of the '12th Five Year Plan'.

Based on the Chinese economic growth rate continuing to be around 7 to 8 per cent per year over the next ten years, Chinese retail sales will continue to grow rapidly in real terms, making the Chinese consumer an increasingly important engine of global economic growth as the size of the Chinese economy converges towards that of the US and European Union.

There is considerable evidence that Chinese private consumption is now already showing significant positive momentum. In 2011, Chinese nominal retail sales rose by around 17 per cent year on year, reflecting the very strong growth in consumer spending.

The increasing global power of Chinese consumer demand is well reflected in the automotive sector, with China having become

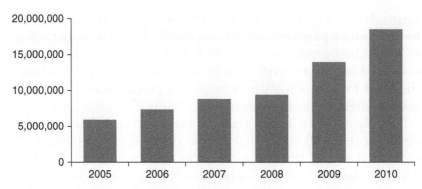

Figure 2.2   Chinese auto sales, number of cars
Source: Chinese Auto Industry Association statistics.

the world's largest auto market in 2009, overtaking the US. The
Chinese auto sector then followed up on this achievement with
spectacular further auto sales growth of 35 per cent in 2010. The
rising spending power of the Chinese consumer is also demonstrated by the rapid growth in premium auto sales in China, which
rose by 77 per cent in 2010.

In the view of one of China's business leaders in the consumer
goods industry, the outlook for Chinese consumer demand remains
very positive. According to Liang Xinjun, Vice Chairman and CEO
of the Fosun Group, a leading Chinese conglomerate, the Chinese
consumer market will grow very strongly over the coming decades.
Liang Xinjun and I were both speakers at the Horasis Global China
Business Meeting in Luxembourg at the end of 2010, and he projected that 'Within ten years, China will become the world's largest
consumer market. If China's GDP grows at between 7 and 8 per
cent per year over the next five to ten years, domestic demand will
grow at 15 per cent per year, with demand for branded goods growing even more quickly, at around 20 per cent per year.'

China will certainly face challenges in rebalancing the structure of the economy away from export-led growth and investment
towards domestic demand, and this transition will take many
years. However, the long-term rise of Chinese consumer demand
is well under way, and is creating a new growth engine for the
global economy at a time when one of the world's key traditional
growth engines, the EU, is mired in a protracted economic crisis.
Strong growth in Chinese consumption will also help to gradually
reduce China's trade imbalances over the medium-term outlook,
as rapid growth in consumer imports results in a narrowing trade

surplus, reducing international frictions over trade imbalances and the yuan exchange rate.

India's rise

While the Indian economy is still significantly smaller than that of China, and its per capita GDP income levels are also much lower, at around one-third of China's, India is still a major consumer market with tremendous future potential.

The total size of the Indian retail market is estimated at around USD 500 billion at present, but the organised retail sector remains small, with considerable potential for rapid growth for global brands.

The Indian government has been very slow to open up this sector to foreign investment, but there have been some significant changes recently which have opened up the Indian market for foreign firms. The decision by the Indian government to allow 100 per cent foreign ownership for single brand retail came into effect in January 2012. However, for FDI involving over 51 per cent ownership, local sourcing of at least 30 per cent is required, which could be a deterrent to some international brands considering the full ownership route.

Many international brands already had JVs in India prior to the decision, but this decision will allow some global brands to accelerate their investment plans for the fast-growing Indian market. International brands such as LVMH, Samsonite and Swarovski have existing retail presence in India, and Starbucks has just announced a joint venture with India's Tata Group to open fifty cafes in India within its first year.

According to US–India International Business Council estimates, the Indian single brand retail market size is currently USD 7 billion, but is expected to triple in size by 2015. The potential liberalisation of the multi-brand retail market is an even bigger overall market opportunity for foreign retail firms, which the government has said it wishes to pursue. The organised retail brand sector is expected to grow very quickly in the next decade.

India's middle class is growing very rapidly, with an estimated 20 million new entrants into the ranks of the Indian middle class each year. This offers tremendous opportunities for global multinationals as well as Indian companies, with the Indian consumer expected to become the next global growth driver for world consumption after China.

Other Asian markets

The sheer size of the population in China and India, which exceeds one billion persons in each country, together with the rapid growth in the size of their middle classes makes these two economies the key drivers of the global shift in consumer demand growth from the OECD countries to emerging markets. However, there are other important fast-growing consumer markets in Asia.

After China and India, Indonesia is also a very large consumer market that is growing rapidly. With a total population of 240 million and a middle class estimated at around 50 million to 100 million persons, depending on what measure of spending power is used, Indonesia is also a key market for global multinationals. This is reflected in the significant investment being made by Japanese auto manufacturers in Indonesia, which has become one of the leading auto manufacturing hubs of Asia, with strong growth in Indonesian demand for automobiles and motorcycles.

Thailand has also become a major Asian auto production hub, helped by the strong growth in both domestic demand and regional demand in other ASEAN countries. The implementation of the ASEAN Free Trade Agreement in 2010 provided a significant boost to Thailand's auto industry, with tariffs on trade in goods within ASEAN largely removed for the first six ASEAN members, while the remaining four will also implement the free trade rules by 2015.

The ten member countries of ASEAN are becoming another major driver of Asian consumer demand. Indeed, the total size of ASEAN GDP is already significantly larger than Indian GDP. Rapid growth in the most populous ASEAN economies of Indonesia and Vietnam will result in strong growth in consumer spending over the medium to long term.

The middle-income economies of Malaysia and Thailand are also attractive due to their higher average per capita incomes and significant spending capacity across a wide spectrum of consumer products, ranging from automobiles to luxury goods. The financial services sector is also benefiting from this rapid growth in consumer spending power, with strong growth in demand for wealth management services as well as other financial services such as insurance.

The new European relationship with Asia

Paris is a beautiful city, and all the praise and accolades lavished on Paris are well deserved. In January 2012, I was visiting Paris to give a speech at a business conference. One morning I had breakfast with a business journalist from one of France's leading daily newspapers. The interview became very interesting when we discussed the future impact of Asia's economic ascent on Europe. The journalist spoke to me of the fears of Asian competition that had been gripping a large share of the French population and would be a key policy issue for the upcoming national elections, namely that low Asian wages would continue to erode French industry and eat away at French jobs. I showed him a French magazine from the hotel's dining room newspaper shelf, which had a blaring headline asking whether Europe needed to revert to protectionist policies to defend its industries.

'This is wrong-headed,' I told him. 'The future economic outlook for European consumption is for low growth. The world has changed. For the last thirty years, it was US and European consumption that was driving global demand and driving the export-led growth model of East Asia. For the next thirty years, it will be consumer demand from emerging markets that will be the key driver of global consumption growth, led by China and India, as well as other large emerging markets such as Brazil, Indonesia and Turkey.' The evidence was all around us – half the tables in the large dining room of the five-star hotel were filled with elegantly dressed Asian customers, predominantly Chinese. Case closed.

For Europe, the rise of Asia undoubtedly has created competitive pressures and the erosion of some segments of industry, such as low value added manufacturing. However, protectionism would be a road to an even greater long-term economic disaster for Europe than has already engulfed it since the financial crisis of 2008–09. What exactly do they want to protect? The European consumer market is going to show very weak growth at best for years to come, as Europe grapples with fiscal consolidation to resolve its sovereign debt crisis combined with the impact of demographic ageing in some European countries such as Italy. The European banks have been deleveraging since 2008, and the outlook for European credit is also likely to be very difficult for years ahead, adding further headwinds to the European growth outlook. Amidst the sea of economic difficulties confronting Europe, Asia offers long-term opportunities.

As can be seen from the quote at the beginning of this chapter, according to the Prime Minister of Luxembourg, Jean-Claude Juncker, Europe's 21st century will be increasingly tied to the emerging market economies.

Juncker is absolutely right in his assessment. The opportunities created for Europe by the rise of Asia are already evident. For example, take the case of the Chinese executives buying watches in Zürich that I described earlier. That is no isolated incident. On any day of the week, large numbers of Chinese and Indian tourists can be found frequenting the watch shops of the touristic destinations of Switzerland. I never fail to be amazed by the throngs of Chinese tourist groups shopping for watches at the shopping and restaurant complex at the top of Mount Titlis, one of Switzerland's most scenic mountains. There is a watch shop in the complex, and it always seems to be full of Chinese tourists buying watches. To get to the top of Mount Titlis, which is 3,238 metres above sea level, takes three separate cable car rides, and the cable car ticket is far from cheap. Once at the top, the Swiss head for the pistes with their fashionable ski outfits or drink hot glühwein and coffees laced with schnapps in the outdoor café in the freezing cold. The Americans and Japanese walk on the snow-covered slopes, throw snowballs and take photos, while the Chinese buy watches.

The Indians also visit in large numbers, and can enjoy authentic vegetarian Indian cooking by specially recruited Indian chefs in the mountaintop restaurant. Indians like Swiss watches too, and the Swiss watch brand Longines used India's famous Bollywood actress and former Miss World Aishwarya Rai as their brand model, while Bollywood hunk Hrithik Roshan has become brand ambassador for Swiss watch company Rado. In 2011, the famous Chinese tennis player Li Na signed an endorsement deal with Rolex. Leading European luxury brands are increasingly using Asian brand ambassadors because they recognise that Asian markets will be key growth drivers for their global revenues in the decades ahead.

Asian tourists are also having a significant impact on total spending on brand names in Europe, with a considerable share of new business at flagship brand stores in the major European capitals coming from spending by emerging market tourists, especially from Asia. A Hong Kong friend complained to me recently that during his holiday in Paris, he gave up waiting to pay for his purchases of French brand items due to the huge number of Asian tourists ahead of him in the queues for the cashiers.

To describe the impact of Asia in the more traditional language of the dry economist, Asian tourism is providing a significant off-set to the negative shock of the European economic crisis. For the Swiss tourism industry in 2011, as the sovereign debt crisis escalated in the European Union, European visitor nights fell by 7 per cent for the Swiss hotel industry. However, in sharp contrast, Chinese visitor nights in Swiss hotels rose by a whopping 47 per cent in 2011, reaching a total of 595,264 nights, making China the sixth largest tourism source for Switzerland. By 2020, the Swiss National Tourist Office projects that total annual Chinese visitor nights will hit the 2 million mark, almost four times higher than in 2011. It seems that Swiss watch shops are going to get considerably busier! And where will these watches be made? Switzerland, of course – nobody is going to come to Switzerland and buy anything other than a genuine 'Made in Switzerland' watch. Swiss watch exports rose 19 per cent in 2011, to reach USD 21 billion, driven by rapid growth in exports to Asia. Half of the total Swiss watch shipments were to Asia, with exports to Hong Kong, the biggest market in the world for Swiss watches, rising by 28 per cent in 2011, while exports to mainland China, the third largest market, rose 49 per cent.

The rapid growth in Asian consumer demand is also becoming increasingly significant for the European Union member countries. EU exports of goods to China rose from 26 billion euro in 2000 to 113 billion euro by 2010, with a further 20 per cent rise in EU exports to China in 2011, to reach a level of 136 billion euro. EU exports of services to China amounted to a further 24 billion in 2011. Overall, China has become increasingly important to the EU export market. In 2000, China accounted for only 3 per cent of total EU exports, while by 2011 its share had trebled to around 9 per cent of total EU exports. To highlight the impact of China as a market for the EU, total EU exports to China are about equivalent to the size of Hungary's GDP at present. If the rapid pace of EU export growth to China continues until 2015, then EU exports to China will exceed Ireland's GDP. This does not include the EU exports to the rest of Asia.

Germany has been the most successful EU country in tapping the Chinese market, with German exports accounting for 48 per cent of total EU exports to China in 2011. France and Italy are the two next biggest EU exporters to China, followed by the UK.

However, many EU countries have not yet positioned themselves for the new gold rush from the Asian ascendancy. Spain and

Portugal stand out as two countries with a history of international trade which seem to have fared rather miserably in readjusting to the changing global economic order. Given the Portuguese seafaring and trading history in Asia, with its establishment of trading posts across Asia in the 16th and 17th centuries, with Portuguese trading ports in Goa and Macau, it is quite remarkable that Portuguese exports to Asia in the calendar year to October 2011 were less than Romanian exports to Asia.

Spain, which is one of the five biggest EU economies, had exports to Asia in the year to October 2011 that were well below Swedish exports to Asia, and only slightly better than Austrian or Finnish exports to Asia. I realised that the Spanish had considerable difficulties in interacting with Asians when I attended the Asian Development Bank annual meeting held in Madrid in 2008. At this meeting, which the Spanish government had presumably hosted in order to foster trade and investment partnerships with Asia, Spanish government officials and business executives tended to form huddles among themselves in the networking opportunities during meals and breaks, seemingly reluctant to interact with their Asian visitors. I wondered whether this was a linguistic problem, but found that most of the Spanish delegates spoke very good English. I remain rather baffled by the whole situation, although it does seem to be reflected in the weak trading relationship Spain has with Asia, as echoed in the trade data.

As teachers are wont to scribble on children's school report cards, I would summarise the situation by saying that Spain and Portugal 'need to try harder' in fostering their economic ties with Asia. Within the EU, Germany is clearly 'top of the class' in having built up its trade and investment relationships with Asia over decades. The German government had already started its strategic engagement with Asia to build economic and investment ties two decades ago, with a major foreign policy push to increase the German government's commercial and trade presence in key economies such as China and Japan. France and Italy are also very successful in the Asian market, with a broad range of merchandise exports ranging from the well-known luxury brands to autos and a wide range of other industrial products. France, the UK and Italy also have significant exports of high-technology products to Asia, such as Airbus aircraft and components, Rolls Royce jet engines and military aircraft such as Dassault fighter jets.

At the Singapore Airshow 2012, Airbus forecast that the Asia-Pacific would become the world's largest air transport market over the next twenty years, with the number of passengers transported by Asia-Pacific airlines projected to grow at 5.9 per cent per year for the next twenty years. Airbus also forecast that Asia-Pacific airlines would take delivery of 9,370 commercial jet aircraft with passenger capacity of over 100 persons over the next two decades, with an estimated value of USD 1.3 trillion and accounting for 34 per cent of the total commercial aircraft market in this segment. Airbus estimated that around 38 per cent of their order backlog was from Asia-Pacific orders, reflecting the importance of Asia for the European aircraft industry.

Recent Boeing forecasts also project strong growth in the total Asia-Pacific market for commercial passenger jets, with Asia-Pacific airlines expected to require 12,030 new aircraft between 2012 and 2031, with a total order value of USD 1.7 trillion.

Tourism is sometimes overlooked as a strategic export, but all these planes being bought in Asia are flying increasing numbers of Asian tourists worldwide. Both France and Italy are major beneficiaries of rapidly rising Asian tourism inflows. Fast-growing tourism inflows not only support spending in tourism-related establishments such as hotels and restaurants, but are also increasingly important for sales of luxury brands in their European stores.

The UK, although the fourth largest exporter of goods to Asia amongst the EU-27, may be somewhat underperforming its potential given its own very strong commercial ties and networks in Asia based on its former colonial linkages with many Asian countries.

A key policy concern confronting the UK is the decline of the manufacturing sector, which used to account for around one-third of GDP in the 1970s but now only contributes 12 per cent of UK GDP. In comparison, the manufacturing sector in Germany accounts for over 20 per cent of GDP. The UK's increasing reliance on the services sector, particularly on financial services, was a key economic vulnerability for the UK during the global crisis of 2008–09 and its aftermath. In contrast, Germany's manufacturing sector has been a source of economic strength since 2008, with the competitiveness of German manufacturing continuing to keep the German economy resilient through the economic crisis.

The weak euro is often cited as a key reason for the strong performance of German manufacturing. While that has certainly been helpful to the German manufacturing sector, the weakness of sterling did not even make the dead British manufacturing cat bounce. The strength of German manufacturing runs much

deeper than just the weak euro, and has been based on many
years of workplace reforms and restructuring combined with wage
restraint. Strong growth in German productivity combined with
wage restraint has delivered significant gains in competitiveness
over the last decade. In contrast, some of the Southern European
countries that are facing medium-term structural economic
reform challenges following the EU sovereign debt crisis had very
poor track records for productivity growth in the last decade,
while wages growth was relatively rapid, leaving their industries
increasingly uncompetitive in global markets.

Prior to the global financial crisis, when the EU was showing
steady but moderate economic expansion at around 2 to 3 per cent
per year, perhaps it was more comfortable culturally for the EU
nations to focus on building their trade and investment ties with
each other, especially since the size of the EU consumer market
combined with moderate positive growth made it a very attractive
priority market globally.

However, that strategy is no longer an option, as the most rapid
growth in the global economy over the next three decades will
be in emerging Asia and other developing countries. Meanwhile
the prospects for European consumer demand growth are weak,
due to the impact of the European sovereign debt crisis on the
European growth outlook, medium-term fiscal consolidation, the
ongoing deleveraging of European bank balance sheets and ageing demographics. Many European governments as well as companies now need to go back to the drawing board to figure out
how to reposition their economies for the rapidly changing global
economic landscape.

Many of the largest European multinationals have already
been repositioning their global strategies towards Asia for some
years. For example, luxury brands from Europe continue to
power ahead, with strong profits driven by rapid growth in Asian
demand. Prada SpA achieved a 72 per cent rise in profits in 2011,
with the Asia-Pacific now the largest regional market for the firm.
Prada's sales to emerging Asia rose 42 per cent in 2011, accounting for one-third of total sales. By 2011, Prada had twenty-five
boutiques in China, and eighteen new stores opened in Asia just in
2011 ('Prada's Asia Focus Boosts Results', *Wall Street Journal*, 30th
March 2012).

Hermes International SCA also posted strong growth in 2011,
with a 41 per cent rise in operating income ('Hermes Raises
Dividend as 2011 Profits Jump', Reuters, 22nd March 2011). Sales

in emerging Asia rose 29 per cent in 2011, and Hermes announced plans to open two new factories in France to cope with rising sales.

For the world's largest luxury brands group, the iconic LVMH, emerging Asia now accounts for 27 per cent of total sales, with Japan accounting for another 8 per cent, so that the combined total sales to the Asia-Pacific region were already 35 per cent of total sales in 2011 ('Key Figures 2011', LVMH).

Samsonite SA, which was listed on the Hong Kong Stock Exchange in 2011, also has seen rapid growth in Asian sales, which rose 42 per cent in 2011. China has rapidly become the second largest market for their products, with sales rising by 63 per cent in 2011. The power of the Chinese middle-class consumer is clearly already making itself felt, and is set to rise significantly in the future.

Zegna's revenues hit 1.1 billion euro in 2011, with around 50 per cent of revenue coming from exports to the Asia-Pacific. One measure of the rapid growth of Asian multinationals is that around the boardrooms and halls of power in the Asia-Pacific, increasing numbers of company chairmen and presidents are indeed wearing Zegna.

Chapter 3

Emerging Asian multinationals

A clash of titans

Emerging powers are rising. The strategic and economic weight of the world is shifting towards this region. There is talk about this being the 'Asian Century'; though I am more inclined to call it 'the Asia-Pacific Century'.

President Dr. Susilo Bambang Yudhoyono, President of Indonesia, Speech at the 11th IISS Shangri-La Dialogue, Singapore, June 2012.

Three hundred Spartans

The 2012 Forbes List of 'The World's Billionaires' lists 312 billionaires from the Asia-Pacific region out of an estimated 1,226 billionaires worldwide. These are mostly first generation entrepreneurs from Asia, and are the front line of corporate Asia's rising global competitiveness in the world economy.

Some of these entrepreneurs have become iconic symbols of Asia's rapid economic ascent. Hong Kong tycoon Li Ka-shing, born in 1928 in Guandong province in China, is estimated to be Asia's richest person according to the Forbes List, with assets of around USD 25 billion. Yet he started his life in poverty, unable to finish his schooling due to his family's difficult financial situation after the death of his father. He worked as a junior manual worker in a factory, eventually starting his own business and emerging as a business tycoon.

Two generations later, another Chinese tycoon has a similar rags-to-riches story. Zhang Xin, born into a poor family in Beijing, started her career as a humble worker in a clothing sweat shop in Hong Kong. She saved enough money to buy a one-way ticket to England, and eventually achieved her ambition of getting a degree in the most spectacular fashion, with a first degree from the University of Sussex and then a master's degree from Cambridge University.

But that was only the beginning. The sweat shop factory girl eventually became a real estate entrepreneur with her husband, founding a small start-up company that later became the Soho China property firm. With an estimated net worth of USD 2.7 billion at the age of 46, Zhang Xin has become an iconic figure in China, a youthful and charismatic role model with a social conscience admired by millions of Chinese as well as people from all over the world. She recently estimated that her social media followers on Weibu, which is similar to Twitter, have reached 2.5 million, and growing rapidly.

In India, Azim Premji, the founder of Wipro, has also become an iconic figure for Indians of all generations. He transformed a small sunflower cooking oil company founded by his father which was called Western India Products Limited into an IT software giant. Wipro's annual revenue in 2011 has reached an estimated USD 7 billion, and the company has 120,000 employees worldwide. With an estimated net worth of USD 16 billion according to the Forbes 2012 List of 'The World's Billionaires', he is admired for the high ethical standards he has set in his company, as well as his philanthropy. In the small town of Amalner where Wipro began with its hydrogenated oil processing plant, those villagers who had bought small amounts of Wipro shares to support the vegetable oil plant and the economic development of their village have seen their wealth soar after Wipro became an IT company.

When I had the opportunity to chair a round-table lunch for Mr Premji to give his views on the business outlook to some senior executives from leading multinationals in the Asia-Pacific, he made a deep impression on me with his humility and thoughtfulness. In addition to his hectic business schedule which involves a high share of global travel to his firm's global offices and key clients worldwide, he also has devoted considerable time and billions of dollars from his personal wealth to philanthropic causes, particularly improving access to education in rural India. It is said that he generally flies economy class on commercial airlines, which, given the intense international travel schedule he must have, is most admirable. How many global business leaders, let alone billionaires, would be willing to do that?

Interestingly, he told me Wipro still manufactures cooking oil and soaps, a business which, he mentioned, still remains profitable. Perhaps there may be another motivation – possibly it works to retain a sense of the simple village roots of the company, to instil humility amongst its fast-growing ranks of high-flying employees.

In a nation where a large share of the population still lives in extreme poverty, many Indian entrepreneurs are perceived by the general public to lead extravagant, nouveaux riche life-styles in a style reminiscent of the worst excesses of the French aristocracy before the French Revolution. Worse still, some of the most well-known business leaders have become embroiled in various corruption scandals in recent years. This has made Azim Premji's ethical standards and high benchmarks for corporate governance even more iconic for ordinary Indians, as well as setting a leading example for other emerging entrepreneurs to follow.

Another Indian icon who is a self-made billionaire from the IT sector is Narayana Murthy, the co-founder of Infosys. His high standards of corporate governance and his humility have also made him one of the most admired business leaders in Asia, with honours bestowed upon him by many governments.

While only some of the 315 Asia-Pacific billionaires today have reached such iconic status among the general public, nevertheless the large number of very wealthy entrepreneurs reflects the rising corporate empires being built in the Asia-Pacific. Few of these business empires existed, at least not on any such global scale, just fifty years ago. Behind the front ranks of the 'Three hundred Spartans' are many thousands of emerging entrepreneurs in Asia whose assets are measured in tens of millions of US dollars and whose companies are fast growing.

This is especially the case in China, where the fast-growing economy and demand for industrial and consumer products by both domestic and global markets has catalysed a tremendous wave of new entrepreneurs.

> En 2011, Shanghai est restée rouge. Rouge Ferrari.
> (In 2011, Shanghai is still red. Ferrari Red.) From 'Chine
> L'effrayante réussite', Erich Follath and Wieland Wagner,
> L'Hebdo, 6th July 2011, from an original article
> in Der Spiegel.

The rising numbers of wealthy Chinese entrepreneurs has indeed given red capitalism a hue of Ferrari red, with Ferrari reporting a 63 per cent increase in the number of cars it sold in Greater China in 2011, making it the world's second largest market for Ferrari cars after the US. This follows a 50 per cent increase in Ferrari sales to China in 2010. Sales to China have soared since the first Ferrari sales to the mainland in 2004, when total annual sales were only 42. By 2011, the Greater China market for Ferrari

Table 3.1 Number of Asia-Pacific billionaires by economy, 2012

China (Mainland)	95
India	48
Hong Kong	38
Taiwan	24
Japan	24
Australia	18
South Korea	20
Indonesia	17
Malaysia	9
Philippines	6
Singapore	5
Thailand	5
New Zealand	3
Asia-Pacific Total	312

Source: Forbes Asia, 'The World's Billionaires', Special Issue, 2012.

cars had reached 777 units. Perhaps this is how China is helping to bail Italy out of its sovereign debt crisis!

The very large increase in the number of Asian billionaires in the last decade reflects the significant growth by Asian multinationals as they expand in fast-growing Asian consumer and industrial markets, as well as growing their global footprint.

A clash of titans

For decades since the end of the Second World War, multinationals from OECD countries dominated the ranks of the world's largest businesses. The main concentration of global top 500 MNCs in Asia was in Japan until very recently. However, there is a rapid change in the structure of the global MNC landscape currently underway. Based on the Fortune Global 500 rankings of the world's largest companies, the share of multinationals from Asian emerging markets in the world's top 500 MNCs has risen significantly since 2005.

In 2005, there were only 107 Asia-Pacific multinationals ranked among the world's top 500 according to the Fortune Global 500 ranking by revenue, with by far the largest share being from Japan. Just six years later, in 2011, the number of APAC multinationals in the Fortune Global 500 list had risen to 171.

This represents a very significant shift within a period of only six years, reflecting the rapid ascendancy of emerging market

Table 3.2   From West to East: the rise of Asian MNCs

	Country	MNCs in Fortune Global 500
	2005	**2011**
Asia-Pacific		
Japan	81	68
China	16	61
Taiwan	2	8
South Korea	11	14
India	5	8
Australia	9	8
Singapore	1	2
Malaysia	1	1
Thailand	1	1
G-7 Western countries		
US	176	133
UK	37	30
France	39	35
Germany	37	34
Italy	8	10
Canada	13	11

Source: Fortune Global 500 List, 2005 and 2011.

Asian multinationals. The key driver for this change has been the rapid growth in the number of Chinese multinationals in the top 500, but the number of Taiwanese, Korean and Indian companies in the ranks of the world's largest companies has also risen significantly.

Meanwhile the total number of multinationals from the G-7 countries has declined over the same period, with the number of US multinationals falling sharply, from 176 in 2005 to 133 by 2011. The number of Japanese, UK, German, French and Canadian multinationals in the Global 500 has also fallen. The only G-7 country which has managed to buck this trend with a rise in the number of its MNCs amongst the global leaders is – rather surprisingly – Italy.

Over the next decade to 2020, it is highly likely that the number of Asian MNCs in the Global 500 list will rise significantly further, as more Chinese, Indian, Korean and Malaysian multinationals enter the ranks of the top global firms.

The competitive landscape in Asia is changing quickly, as Asian multinationals increasingly capture market share in a wide range of industries in the Asia-Pacific. The strongest competitive impact is likely to come from the fast-growing companies in China and India, which have sustained double digit revenue growth in their domestic markets due to the large size of their home country populations and the rapid growth in consumer spending over the next twenty years.

This will help to generate strong growth in profits and expansion in the size of corporate balance sheets in the most successful Asian multinationals, creating increasing balance sheet capability to expand into regional markets over time. The capacity of these firms to use capital markets financing to undertake both domestic and cross-border acquisitions to expand their market share will also increase.

As a result, OECD multinationals will face rising competitive pressures in key growth markets, particularly in the Asia-Pacific. In addition, there will be an uptrend in mergers and acquisitions activity by Asian multinationals, as they become more aggressive in acquiring companies in a wide range of industries.

The resources sector will become an increasingly important area of such activity for both Chinese and Indian firms, as they seek to acquire control of resources in order to supply their rapidly rising requirements for energy, metals and agricultural commodities. While this trend of rising resource-related acquisitions by Chinese and Indian companies has already been evident over the last decade, it will continue to increase over the next twenty years. This is likely to become the source of political friction in many commodity-exporting countries, as domestic concerns rise about large-scale control of some of their key resources by foreign firms, particularly if large shares of a commodity are under the control of a single foreign country.

In manufacturing, similar trends will occur, as developing country multinationals seek to acquire market share as well as technology and innovative processes through acquisition. This is already evident in the automotive industry with acquisitions by Chinese auto firm Zhejiang Geely Holding Group Co. Ltd. of Volvo Cars, and the acquisition by India's Tata Motors of Jaguar Land Rover.

Zhejiang Geely Holding Group Co. Ltd., a large Chinese auto manufacturer headquartered in Hangzhou, bought Volvo Cars from Ford Motor in 2010 for USD 1.8 billion. In March 2012, Zhejiang Geely and Volvo announced they had signed a technology transfer agreement which would involve joint development of electric cars and hybrid technology.

The acquisition of Jaguar Land Rover by Tata Motors in 2008 has proved to be highly successful. With rapid expansion in

Table 3.3   Large cross-border acquisitions by Indian firms

Year	Indian Firm	Foreign Target	Cost (in USD bn)
2007	Tata Steel	Corus	13.3
2007	Hindalco	Novelis	6.2
2008	Tata Motors	Jaguar Land Rover	2.3
2009	ONGC	Imperial Energy	2.1
2010	Bharti Airtel	Zain Africa	10.7

Sources: *The Economist*, 3rd March 2012; *Indian Express*, 24th March 2011.

demand for the Jaguar and Land Rover cars, particularly from emerging markets, the JLR workforce in the UK is already 19,000 strong. Furthermore, its activities are estimated to support an additional 140,000 jobs in the UK. In September 2011, Tata Motors announced that a new engine plant would be built in the UK for GBP 355 million, which was estimated to require around 900 new jobs.

Red capitalism – China's 'go global' policy

While the acquisition of foreign companies by Indian companies has been largely driven by the Indian private sector, with some state-owned companies acquiring energy assets, the situation is different in China. Large state-owned enterprises still play a prominent role in many sectors of the Chinese economy, and therefore the role of state policy has been a significant factor in the cross-border acquisitions strategy of Chinese firms.

During the past decade, there have been progressive measures to support increasing foreign direct investment by Chinese firms. From a government policy perspective, the framework for a national strategy for Chinese companies to become more international was set in place. Key strategic objectives of this strategy were to improve resource security by acquiring access to foreign resources, as well as to acquire leading-edge technology to boost the competitiveness of Chinese industry.

The broad strategy was supported by measures to provide financial assistance to firms wishing to invest abroad. Subsequent liberalisation measures included removing foreign exchange quotas for foreign investment in 2006, and regulatory reforms by the banking regulator in 2008 to allow Chinese state-owned banks to provide loans for cross-border mergers and acquisitions activity by Chinese companies.

These reforms have been facilitated by the very rapid growth in Chinese foreign exchange reserves over the last decade, due to sustained large trade surpluses as well as large capital inflows from foreign direct investment. This has provided large-scale pools of foreign exchange to support China's internationalisation policy.

In the first decade of China's increasing foreign acquisitions activity there have already been some significant, high-profile cases when intended acquisitions have been rejected by foreign governments due to concerns about the strategic implications of China acquiring control of key companies in certain sectors.

In the US, CNOOC's USD 18.4 billion bid for Unocal in 2005 was withdrawn after fierce political opposition in the US. In Australia, there was also considerable political controversy over a bid by a Chinese state-owned firm, Chinalco, for Rio Tinto, which would have given the Chinese firm control over a considerable part of Western Australia's vast iron ore deposits. However, the bid was rejected after BHP Billiton and Rio agreed to a deal to share their iron ore reserves in Western Australia.

As China continues to pursue its resource security objectives over the long-term to address its energy security and food security needs, there are likely to be increasing political tensions in other resource-rich countries as well.

The decision by the Indonesian government in March 2012 to restrict foreign ownership in the mining sector to 49 per cent is one example of how governments in resource-rich countries may seek to retain national control over their natural resources. The increasing efforts by Chinese and Indian companies to acquire foreign resources could well trigger a political backlash in other nations where there are strong investment inflows by these two countries into the natural resources sector of a nation. As China and India continue to grow rapidly over the next two decades, these political tensions are likely to intensify in resource-exporting countries.

The rise of other economic powers since the Second World War has triggered similar reactions. During the 1960s and 1970s, there was a political backlash in many countries to the rising economic dominance of the US and the expanding global role of US multinationals. In the 1980s, there was mounting paranoia in the US about the rise of Japan as an economic power, and the volume of Japanese corporate acquisitions in the US.

However, if China does reclaim its historic importance in the world economy, this will imply a very significant increase in its economic role in global trade and investment. It seems inevitable that this will create rising political fears amongst governments and the general public in many resource-exporting nations about the increasingly dominant economic role of China in their resources sector, as a key investor in their natural resources and the largest export market. A significant backlash against Chinese and also perhaps Indian ownership of natural resources in other developing countries is probable, and more developing countries are likely to adopt measures to restrict foreign ownership in their resources economy and other strategic industry sectors.

Technology wars of the future

Technology, research and development as well as innovation will become increasingly important drivers of competitive advantage in coming decades in a wide range of key manufacturing and service industries. In the last five decades, technological leadership has continued to be an important driver of competitive advantage for US and European multinationals. However, the global competitive landscape is changing.

One key structural change is the significantly improved educational infrastructure in China and India, with large numbers of graduates in science and engineering each year. This has driven a significant shift in the location of global R&D facilities towards China and India, due to the large pool of highly qualified scientists and engineers.

As Asian multinationals grow in size of revenue and also expand their global operations, it is likely that they will also put increased strategic focus on R&D and innovation. Japanese and Korean IT and auto MNCs have already done this for decades, but the emerging markets MNCs from China and India are also increasing their strategic focus on R&D and innovation in order to build their competitive advantage. An important focus of the mergers and acquisitions strategy of Chinese and Indian MNCs is to acquire technology, as occurred in the landmark M&A deals by Zhejiang Geely to acquire Volvo Cars and by Tata Motors to buy Jaguar Land Rover. Supported by their highly capable tertiary qualified workforces, this gives Asian multinationals considerable potential to become leaders in technology and innovation over the next two decades.

Table 3.4 Asia-Pacific region R&D expenditure, 2008, % of GDP

By:	Business	Government	Gross
Singapore	1.9	0.9	2.8
China	1.1	0.4	1.5
India	0.4	0.6	1.0
Malaysia	0.4	0.3	0.7
Japan	2.6	0.6	3.4
South Korea	2.5	0.9	3.4
OECD	1.6	0.7	2.3

Sources: National government statistics; OECD data; World Bank data.

The competition between Asia and the West for technological leadership will intensify over coming decades due to the growing size of Asian multinationals, as well as the increasing focus of many Asian governments from a policy perspective to boost national competitiveness in R&D as well as in innovation. Asian economies which have moved into middle-income status are compelled to increasingly focus on technology and R&D, as their manufacturing sectors need to develop higher value-added production and exports if they are to remain competitive globally as wage costs rise.

Recent R&D estimates for some of Asia's largest economies show that R&D spending does still vary significantly amongst Asian industrial economies. Nevertheless, overall R&D spending as a share of GDP is very high in Japan, South Korea and Singapore, with all three countries having R&D spending that exceeds the OECD average by a significant proportion.

Moreover, the total amount of R&D dollars spent in Asia is increasingly large, due to the rapidly growing size of the major Asian economies. Official figures released by the Chinese Ministry of Science and Technology estimate that Chinese R&D spending had risen to 1.76 per cent of GDP by 2010, an increase of 21.7 per cent compared to the previous year. Total R&D spending was estimated at RMB 706 billion. The greatest intensity of R&D spending in China has been concentrated in six provinces, which accounted for around 60 per cent of total R&D spending in 2010. These were Beijing, Shanghai, Guangdong, Tianjin, Shaanxi and Zhejiang.

While total US R&D spending, which was estimated at around USD 400 billion in 2009, still far exceeds Chinese R&D spending by a factor of around 4:1, total Chinese R&D spending is projected to converge towards that of the US over the next decade. A key factor driving this convergence is that average US R&D

spending has been growing at around 5 per cent per year over the last decade, while Chinese R&D spending has been growing at around 20 per cent per year. Moreover, whereas the US government is now facing a decade of budget spending cuts in order to try to reduce government debt levels, the Chinese government's debt burden, albeit moderately high after taking into account contingent liabilities for local government debt, is not yet a constraint on budget expenditure increases for key policy priorities such as R&D.

If these trends in US and Chinese R&D spending continue for the next decade, then Chinese R&D convergence will be very rapid. Indeed, in just one decade, Chinese R&D spending in terms of total US dollars of spending will exceed the US based on current exchange rates. Should the Chinese yuan appreciate to any significant extent against the US dollar over the next decade, then the catch-up in USD terms will be even more rapid.

A key assumption underlying these projections over the next decade is that the trend growth rates for R&D spending for China and the US remain the same as in the recent past over the next decade. There are certainly good reasons to be cautious about the scope for US R&D spending growth rates to be higher on average in the next decade than they were over the past decade, given the significant US government spending cuts that are targeted over the next decade as well as their implications for the defence sector, which accounts for a high share of total US R&D.

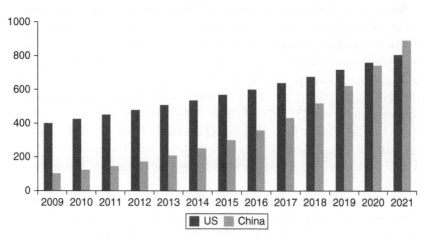

Figure 3.1 R&D Spending in the US and China, USD billion
Source: Author's projections.

However, isn't it too optimistic to assume that Chinese R&D spending growth rates can keep up a 20 per cent pace each year for another ten years? If one assumes that Chinese GDP can grow at around 8 per cent per year over the next decade, which is already 2 per cent lower annual average growth than over the last two decades, and also take into account the significant growth of Chinese MNCs currently taking place, with a strong policy priority at national level to boost R&D spending to gain technological competitiveness and move up the value-adding chain, then perhaps such high growth rates are not too ambitious. These assumptions also do not allow for any further yuan appreciation against the USD over the next ten years, so if some appreciation is also assumed then the USD value of Chinese R&D spending would also rise more rapidly. However, these assumptions are for a ten-year horizon, and beyond that the pace of Chinese R&D growth would most likely slow significantly due to the impact of ageing demographics and declining marginal productivity of capital on GDP growth rates, as the overall pace of Chinese economic growth slips below 7 per cent in the decade beyond 2022.

Nevertheless, over the next decade, rapid technological convergence should be expected as China puts a high strategic policy priority on R&D and technology. Based on the expectation that the Chinese economy will become the world's largest economy by around 2025, then rapid convergence of Chinese R&D spending with that of the US economy is very likely to occur. With Chinese GDP projected to significantly outstrip the US over the decade beyond 2025, the total size of Chinese R&D spending is on a trajectory to overtake the US.

Whether or not this happens precisely by 2021 or several years later, the strategic implications are the same. The dominance of global R&D and technological capability by the US and Europe since the time of the Industrial Revolution is now rapidly eroding, and Asia's role in global technological leadership seems destined to rise quickly over the next two decades, driven by the growing relative share of Asia in world GDP as well as the ascendancy of Asian multinationals as global corporate leaders.

While the increasing role of China in global technology spending is a key driver of Asia's rise, other Asian countries are also giving a high policy priority to R&D, with South Korea being a leading example. In 2010, South Korean R&D spending rose by an estimated 15.6 per cent, according to government figures, with total R&D spending reaching around USD 40 billion.

This is around one-tenth of current US R&D spending, but if double digit growth in South Korean R&D spending continues for another decade, even at a more conservative trend growth rate of 10 per cent per year, then South Korean R&D spending would reach around one-fifth that of the US, assuming the US does not manage to increase its own R&D spending growth rate.

However, there are strong impediments to the ability of the US government and corporate sector to accelerate R&D spending. Firstly, the US government faces a decade of significant spending constraints and the need to lower the overall government debt as a share of GDP, which will restrict US government funding for R&D. Secondly, a large share of R&D spending is related to defence, and this is also a key sector facing spending cuts over at least the next decade. Thirdly, private sector firms are increasingly looking to outsource R&D to emerging markets, albeit in captive R&D centres, in order to tap lower wage costs for highly skilled scientists and IT specialists, as well as due to the far greater supply of new scientific graduates in countries such as China and India.

Therefore the shape of global technology and research is rapidly changing, with Asia set to become the world's leading technology and R&D hub within a decade. This trend is being driven by a range of factors, including the high policy priority that China, South Korea, Singapore and Taiwan are giving to R&D spending and the related development of higher education institutions to provide a sufficient supply of highly skilled science and technology graduates. However, the ascent of Asian multinationals is also playing a key role, as the increasing number of Asian MNCs in the ranks of the world's largest firms is also reshaping the ownership of global private sector R&D spending.

Yet the Asian R&D landscape is hardly homogenous. Whereas China, South Korea and Singapore are putting a high government policy focus on technology and R&D spending as a share of GDP is higher in Japan, South Korea and Singapore than the OECD average, other countries are laggards. In particular, it is notable that estimated Indian R&D spending is significantly lower than North Asian countries, both in the private and government sectors. To a significant extent this reflects the weakness of the Indian government's technology policies as well as the high government debt levels, which constrain the ability of the government to boost government spending on R&D. However, it also reflects the weakness of the economic policy environment for encouraging R&D through the types of government incentives and fiscal topography that exists in many OECD and emerging Asian countries that have a better track record on R&D. The more dynamic segments of Indian industry such as the IT, pharma and auto sectors are showing more rapid growth in R&D spending in the last decade, and this trend will likely boost overall private sector R&D growth rates over coming decades. Nevertheless, the weakness of the government's technology policy remains a key obstacle to India's economic development.

Malaysia is suffering from a similar technology deficit, with overall R&D spending as a share of GDP of only around 0.7 per cent, which is less than one-third of the OECD average. As Malaysia is a middle-income developing country whose manufacturing sector needs to rapidly move up the value-adding chain in order to maintain international competitiveness, this low R&D spending is a key policy concern. The Malaysian government's 'Economic Transformation Programme' announced in 2010 has included new strategies to try to boost Malaysia's technological capabilities, but this will be a long process involving significant change in many segments of the economy, including the higher education sector, research institutes and private corporations, as Malaysia tries to create clusters of excellence in various areas of industry R&D.

Leadership challenges for Asian MNCs

Western MNCs have had many decades of global operating experience to develop their global talent management and leadership models. In the Asia-Pacific, most of the largest Western MNCs have very multicultural senior leadership teams managing their Asia-Pacific operations. As I have frequently been invited to speak to the Asia-Pacific senior leadership teams of many US and European Fortune Global 500 MNCs, I can say from firsthand experience that the Asia-Pacific senior leadership teams of these large multinationals are usually highly diverse. Nationals from many Asian countries are usually seated at the boardroom table, alongside their Western counterparts from the US and Europe. When I speak to these Asian senior executives, they have invariably had extensive careers with their firm or other MNCs with blue-chip credentials. The value that these diverse cultural and professional backgrounds bring to the table is obvious in the discussions.

Where Western MNCs have had less vision is in creating more international leadership at the headquarters level and in their boardrooms, with a prevailing bias towards more homogenous compositions of senior leadership. This creates significant weaknesses in strategic vision and global decision-making for large Western MNCs which need to seek revenue growth in emerging market regions. There are signs of gradual change as US and European MNCs slowly accept the need to have more emerging markets expertise in their boardrooms and amongst their headquarters' leadership teams.

However, Asian MNCs that have entered relatively recently into the big league of global MNCs often have significantly less experience of running global operations. Consequently they face a more difficult transition towards adopting more international management and board structures.

Chinese state-owned enterprises have in some ways been amongst the most forward-looking in this regard. While it is often difficult for a state-owned enterprise in many countries to appoint non-nationals to their board or senior management, a number of the key Chinese state-owned enterprises have established international advisory councils comprising international business leaders and academics to advise them on global strategic trends and policies. Some of the Chinese organisations that have established international advisory councils include China Investment Corporation, which is China's sovereign wealth fund, China Development Bank, the Chinese banking regulator China Banking Regulatory Commission, and Huawei Technologies Co. Ltd., one of China's leading information technology and telecommunications hardware companies.

Singapore also has a number of international advisory councils for key organisations, including for the Monetary Authority of Singapore, the Economic Development Board, the Government of Singapore Investment Corporation and Temasek.

However, emerging market MNCs also face a significant learning curve in appointing more international senior leadership, since they have often had limited global operations and have often not developed global talent management programmes. Therefore, one of the key strategic challenges facing the rapidly growing number of emerging market MNCs will be how to internationalise their senior leadership and top management as they become more global in scope. These MNCs may face significant challenges in this internationalisation of their management culture as they expand their operations globally, including through acquisitions of companies in different regions of the world.

Consequently, these MNCs will need to increasingly focus on the best practice examples of large multinationals which have had a long track record of international operations. Emerging Asian MNCs will need to adopt the ideas and strategies of global MNC standards-setters in the internationalisation of their corporate culture as well as creating global talent management and international leadership teams.

The future global competitive landscape

The rapidly growing numbers of Asian MNCs amongst the Fortune Global 500 reflects the far-reaching changes that are taking place in the global economy. If the momentum of emerging market MNCs continues at the pace seen in the last seven years, then by 2020 it is quite possible that half of the world's largest MNCs will be from Asia. This will create a very different global corporate landscape to that of 1990.

The strategic implications of this transformation are significant.

Firstly, Western MNCs will face ever-increasing competition in global markets, particularly in the fast-growing emerging markets of Asia, the backyard of emerging Asian multinationals. The rise of Chinese multinationals has only just begun, as their fast-growing domestic market has propelled them into global giants that are now positioning themselves to engage in global markets. As emerging market multinationals focus greater efforts on building their global market presence and creating international brands, they will become increasingly powerful competitors for global market share. Strategic acquisitions such as the Tata Motors purchase of Jaguar Land Rover have transformed the brand image and capabilities of Tata Motors to tap global markets compared to just a decade ago.

Secondly, emerging Asian multinationals will increasingly become more powerful competitors in leading-edge technology. This will reflect their ability to fund large-scale R&D programmes from their fast-growing balance sheets, combined with the competitive advantage of having large pools of highly skilled science and technology graduates from their own educational systems.

Thirdly, the war for talent will become more intensified as large emerging market multinationals compete with the Western MNCs for the best technical expertise. In the last fifty years, Western MNCs were able to drive their technological development, R&D centres and innovation strategies with a large pool of low-cost, highly skilled science and technology graduates from Asian countries, notably China, India, Taiwan and South Korea. As Asian MNCs become global leaders and can offer similar compensation packages for talent, it is likely to become much harder to persuade Asian talent to leave their own region to work for Western firms. A clear implication of the rising number of Asian MNCs that are global leaders is that the cost of scientific and technological skills will rise, and Asia will no longer be a cheap source of 'high-tech coolies'.

Fourthly, as Asian MNCs become an increasingly larger share of the global leaders, their impact on the structure of global capital flows will also be more significant. As Asian MNCs become far more important players in global business, their cross-border M&A activity will also expand rapidly, a trend that is already evident in Chinese and Indian outbound M&A flows. This could result in increasing political tensions as well as a regulatory backlash in some countries which fear their economies and key strategic industries may become dominated by one or two large Asian countries. As China's economy becomes the largest in the world over the next two decades, overtaking the US and EU, some of the greatest concerns about China's rising economic dominance will likely emanate from some Asia-Pacific countries.

Chapter 4

The ascent of Asian finance

I invest only when I hear the sound of cannon fire and see blood running in the streets.

Nathan Rothschild,
19th century financier

The evolution of global finance

When Wellington defeated Napoleon at the Battle of Waterloo in 1812, Nathan Rothschild is reputed to have received the news through his own personal messengers more swiftly than the British government. In what has now become a legendary example of his financial acumen, he is believed to have used this advance information together with clever trading tactics to make significant profits by trading in government consols on the London Stock Exchange. The rise of the House of Rothschild during the 19th and 20th centuries has become almost synonymous with the rise of European finance during that era.

The ascendancy of Western finance that led to its global dominance today had its roots in the rise of commerce in the Venetian Empire, and the expansion of financial centres in Renaissance Italy in Florence, Venice and Genoa. European banking became increasingly international in its scope during the Industrial Revolution and the age of European colonialism, despite various European wars, banking crises and sovereign debt defaults. The expansion of the British Empire in the 17th and 18th centuries was accompanied by the rise of British financial institutions, with London becoming the pre-eminent international financial centre by the late 19th century. The rapid economic development of the US after the American Civil War also resulted in New York emerging as a key financial centre.

The dominance of US and European banking continued until the Second World War. The new global financial architecture created at the end of the war at the Bretton Woods Conference in 1944, and constituting the IMF and the IBRD, was also mainly driven by the US and its European allies, with a total of 44 founding member countries.

During the evolution of the Bretton Woods institutions over the next seven decades, the US and European members have continued to dominate the voting rights of the Bretton Woods institutions, despite the significant rise of the share of emerging markets in world GDP. Although developing countries such as China and India have continued to press for larger voting rights over the years, the pace of reform has been very slow, with voting rights still heavily concentrated with the US and Europe.

Moreover, the leadership of the IMF and World Bank has been divided up between the US and Europe since the creation of the Bretton Woods system, with a European always at the helm of the IMF and an American always leading the World Bank. As the membership of the Bretton Woods institutions has continued to expand, growing from 44 founding members to 187 members, with most of the new members from developing countries, the demands from developing countries for a more transparent, inclusive and merit-based approach to the selection of the leadership of the Bretton Woods institutions have continued to grow, but have been stubbornly resisted by the US and Europe.

Despite the decline of colonialism after the end of the Second World War, cross-border international finance continued to be dominated by the banks, insurance companies and asset management firms of North America and Europe for many decades. While the Japanese financial centre grew rapidly as the Japanese economy became the world's second largest economy, the global expansion of Japanese financial institutions ended rapidly after the collapse of the Japanese economy bubble during the 1990s. A decade of deleveraging by Japanese banks resulted in a substantial retreat from international finance and a refocusing on domestic business.

The continued dominant role of the US and European banks has created considerable vulnerabilities for the world economy, as was demonstrated during the financial crisis in 2008–09, due to the freezing up of international money markets and credit markets. The large European and US banks at the heart of international financing experienced severe difficulties in accessing credit after the collapse of Lehman Brothers, causing liquidity problems that forced the sudden and rapid deleveraging of bank balance sheets. This in turn resulted in a massive contraction in international financial flows for developing countries. The sharp decline in availability of international trade finance played a significant role in the slump in world trade that occurred in 2008–09.

With the European sovereign debt crisis continuing to escalate during 2011–12, as contagion has spread from one highly indebted European nation to another, the European banks continue to face a protracted period of deleveraging of bank balance sheets as they continue to try to repair risk-weighted capital ratios. In the US, the massive task of government deficit reduction will be a drag on US economic growth for years to come. Meanwhile, as Asia-Pacific economies and other developing countries continue to grow more rapidly than the OECD region, the asymmetric structure of international finance has created significant vulnerabilities for the financing of economic development in emerging markets.

Building an Asian financial architecture

As Asia's economic ascendancy has continued to increase its share of global GDP, there has been rising discontent in Asia with the current structure of the global financial architecture, which continues to be dominated by the US and Europe.

During the East Asian financial crisis, Japan proposed the creation of an Asian Monetary Fund that would be made up of only Asian countries. This was strongly opposed by the US, which argued that such a regional financial grouping would undermine and dilute the effectiveness of the IMF.

While efforts by Japan to resuscitate the proposal have not yet succeeded, the momentum for a regional Asian financial architecture has continued to gather momentum. A key driver for this has been the evolution of ASEAN as a regional economic grouping. An important turning point in the Asian political landscape regarding a new financial architecture was the Chiang Mai Initiative, which was agreed by the ASEAN countries together with China, Japan and South Korea (ASEAN+3) in May 2000. Initially the Chiang Mai agreement comprised a network of bilateral swap agreements among the member countries, in order to address the types of liquidity vulnerabilities that hit Asian economies during the East Asian crisis.

The Chiang Mai Initiative has evolved over time and, by 2010, the ASEAN+3 members had agreed to a Chiang Mai Initiative Multilateralisation (CMIM). This created a multilateral swap arrangement with a reserve pool of USD 120 billion. However, the CMIM is still very restrictive due to the condition that countries requiring access to the FX facilities could draw down only 20 per cent of their total drawing rights without going to the IMF and accepting IMF conditionality. Therefore the construct of the ASEAN+3 facility had, for all practical purposes, failed to achieve what was presumably its primary purpose, which was to create a regional facility for short-term liquidity problems among its members without recourse to the global IFIs.

However, by restricting members to accessing very small amounts of funding without IMF conditionality, the Chiang Mai Initiative became essentially a paper tiger, unable to fulfil the purpose for which it had been created.

Therefore for now, the facility has remained unused. Given the political distaste in Asia for subjecting their countries to IMF conditionality, countries have preferred to seek other solutions during times of crisis. The greatest recent test for Asia came during the global financial crisis in 2008–09, when South Korea and Indonesia suffered capital flight due to the erosion of confidence of global investors. For South Korea, their large-scale need for US dollars was never going to be met by their Chiang Mai swap arrangements anyway. It was the US Federal Reserve's agreement to provide a USD 30 billion bilateral swap facility that drew the financial markets' heat away from South Korea, as global investors realised the US was going to stand behind South Korea, providing a large flow of USD as needed. This was the beginning of the end of South Korea's FX crisis, as global hedge funds speculating against the Korean won realised they couldn't bet against the Fed.

Clearly the overall regional financial architecture in Asia is still in its early formative stage, but as the economic weight of Asian economies grows, the likelihood that some form of Asian Monetary Fund will eventually be created is growing. Moreover, there is increasing political support within Asia for such a move, albeit still cautious.

Perhaps the key driving force for the creation of an Asian Monetary Fund will be the continued evolution of ASEAN. The goal of ASEAN to create an ASEAN Economic Community by 2015, including reduction of barriers to trade in services and free movement of capital, contains the underlying objective of greater financial integration.

This cannot happen without some form of ASEAN financial forum where central banks and regulators can regularly meet to discuss and manage cross-border regulatory issues. The creation of AMRO is already a step towards the type of financial systems surveillance that is undertaken by the IMF at a global level. Therefore, the likelihood of some form of Asian Monetary Fund being created within the next decade has risen significantly due to the ASEAN agenda. This will be a very positive step forward for the region in terms of strengthening its regional financial architecture, and is long overdue.

Another important step forward will also be the transformation of the Chiang Mai Initiative into a workable facility that can provide regional assistance to individual countries facing FX liquidity crises without automatic linkage to IMF conditionality. ASEAN+3 governments agreed in 2012 to double the size of the CMIM reserve pool to USD 240 billion. They also recognised that there were other important drawbacks limiting the effectiveness of the CMIM and by implication, the ability of Asian governments to mount any kind of effective liquidity support operations to assist a member country.

Importantly, ASEAN+3 governments recognised in their 2012 agreement that the East Asian monetary cooperation exercise could not continue to rely on linking their entire fund operations to IMF conditionality indefinitely. Therefore they created for the first time a share of the total reserve pool that would be available to members without the requirement for IMF conditionality.

Nevertheless, some form of ASEAN+3 conditionality will need to be developed to avoid the problem of moral hazard. Moral hazard is a clear risk when providing funds to countries that have mismanaged their own affairs then draw on large-scale funding from the ASEAN+3 without undertaking necessary reforms. The ASEAN+3 countries certainly have the technical capacity to assemble a highly capable task force to assist member countries with policy advice about necessary economic reforms. Whether they have the political will to impose conditionality is a much thornier question.

Growth of Asia-Pacific banking markets

During the first fifty years since the end of the Second World War, the US and Europe were the largest economic regions of the world economy. The dominance of US and European banks in international finance therefore reflected the weight of their economies in the global economy. The role of US and European banks was also boosted by an era of relatively strong economic growth in the US and Europe. Combined with progressive financial innovation and deregulation of financial markets, this helped to fuel rapid growth in financial services sectors in the US and Europe, resulting in strong growth in their balance sheets, supporting the expansion of their leading positions in international finance.

However, there has been a very rapid and dramatic shift in these trends during the last decade. The growing economic weight of China followed by that of other large emerging economies such as India and Brazil have resulted in a rapid rebalancing of the global economy as the total size of GDP in developing countries is rapidly converging to the total size of GDP in the developed countries. Meanwhile growth in the OECD countries is expected to remain weak over the medium-term, as heavily indebted developed countries struggle with fiscal consolidation.

The rapid growth of the Asia-Pacific region has made it the largest and fastest growing global market for financial services, led by very swift economic growth in China and India, which is driving the rising demand for financial services. However, Asia-Pacific banks, despite their large and fast-growing domestic bank balance sheets, have not yet become significant players in the big league of global finance. While Japanese banks did make significant inroads in international finance during the 1980s, the bursting of the Japanese economic bubble forced a major contraction in the international operations of Japanese banks, as they underwent a decade of restructuring and consolidation to address their own banking crisis.

The asymmetry in international finance is still clearly reflected in investment banking in Asia, with US and European banks

Table 4.1 Investment bank revenues in Asia (ranked by revenue in USD million, year to August 2011)

Bank	Ranked by revenue in USD
Nomura	1st
Morgan Stanley	2nd
Goldman Sachs	3rd
Mizuho	4th
Bank of America Merrill Lynch	5th
UBS	6th
Deutsche Bank	7th
Credit Suisse	8th
Citi	9th

Source: *Wall Street Journal*, 12th August 2011, Dealogic.

continuing to dominate the Asian investment banking business in key areas of international finance, including mergers and acquisitions, international IPOs, international bond placements and syndicated lending. While several Japanese banks are also large players, seven of the nine top investment banks by revenue in 2011 year to date are from the US and Europe.

While international banks from the US and Europe may like to be perceived as globalised in nature, the reality is very different. US and European banks that are major players in international finance remain heavily driven by the economic and regulatory environment in their home markets, with the composition of their boards and top management also strongly reflecting their home base.

The reliance of developing countries on international financing from European and US banks increases their vulnerability to the financial system problems of Europe and the US. This has been clearly demonstrated by the present economic crisis confronting Europe, where many of the large European banks that are major players in international finance have been experiencing protracted deleveraging of their balance sheets since the onset of the global financial crisis in 2008, with problems expected to continue for years to come as the European sovereign debt crisis continues to impact European economic growth as well as capital ratios of banks.

For emerging European economies, this has heightened their vulnerability to the Eurozone sovereign debt crisis. Not only have their economies been hit by the contagion effects of weaker Eurozone growth on trade and investment flows, but also by the transmission effects of deleveraging of bank balance sheets by Western European banks, which had expanded into emerging Europe through acquisitions of domestic banks. With a high share of banking system assets in many emerging European economies now owned by Western European banks, these countries have also been hit by the credit crunch that has engulfed Western European banks in European financial centres such as the UK, Germany, France, Austria and Italy.

For emerging markets, this dependency on international financing from Western banks has resulted in a roller coaster ride of international lending flows by international commercial banks. Periods of rapid expansion in credit have been followed by sharp contraction in international lending, which has had a significant impact on emerging markets by restricting lending for trade and

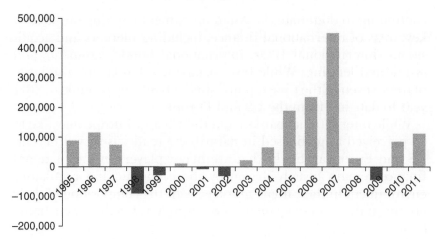

Figure 4.1 International lending by commercial banks to emerging markets, 1995–2011, USD million

Source: Institute of International Finance data.

investment. Such volatility in capital flows creates considerable risks for developing countries in terms of their own economic development, since such extreme volatility of financing flows can significantly disrupt trade and investment flows.

While the share of GDP of developing countries in the global economy is now comparable to the developed countries, and is forecast to significantly surpass developed countries within the next decade, the role of developing countries' financial institutions in international finance remains small.

Therefore, a reshaping of the structure of global finance is needed in order to reduce the vulnerability of developing countries to the economies and financial systems of the US and Europe. This will require a significant expansion in the role of financial institutions from Asia and other emerging market regions in international finance.

Asia's rising role in international finance

In the Asia-Pacific region, there are positive signs that Asian financial houses are beginning to play a greater role in international finance. One important milestone in this diversification has been the opportunistic re-entry by Nomura into international investment banking by acquiring Lehman Brother's Asian, Middle Eastern and European operations in 2008 after the Lehman collapse.

This has transformed Nomura from a firm focused mainly on Japanese domestic business and a very small player in global investment banking into a leading international firm with a strong Asia-Pacific heritage and focus.

In Singapore, large Singaporean banks are increasing their regional footprint, building on their financial strength with sound balance sheets and their robust domestic operations in Singapore. For example, DBS has become a leading financial services group in the region, as it has expanded beyond its well-developed operations in Singapore and Hong Kong. It has significantly built up its Greater China operations in the last five years, with eighteen branches and sub-branches in mainland China and forty distribution outlets in Taiwan. DBS also has twelve branches in India, a branch in Vietnam and has acquired a 99 per cent ownership of its Indonesian subsidiary, PT Bank DBS Indonesia. DBS has also launched the Islamic Bank of Asia, in order to tap the fast-growing markets for Islamic finance in the Middle East and Asia.

Malaysia has also emerged as an increasingly important regional banking player following the consolidation of its banking industry after the East Asian crisis. The Malaysian domestic banking sector has been fundamentally transformed in the last decade, with the financial system very much strengthened by the reform process. Gross non-performing loans as a share of total lending by banks are estimated at around 3.2 per cent in the first quarter of 2011, while the risk-adjusted capital adequacy ratio for the Malaysian banking system is estimated at 14.3 per cent. This has created a strong launching pad for Malaysia's large banking groups to expand regionally.

For example, Malaysia's CIMB Group operates in a number of other economies in ASEAN, with full universal banking operations in Singapore, Indonesia and Thailand, as well as having consumer banking services in Cambodia. CIMB also has operations in other global locations, including other Asian countries and in the Middle East. Malaysia's Maybank also has become an important regional financial services firm in ASEAN, with operations in eight out of the ten ASEAN countries. In Singapore, Maybank is a full licence commercial bank with a large number of branches, and in Indonesia it operates through a syariah bank PT Bank Maybank Syariah Indonesia. Maybank also has a presence in many other countries, including the Philippines, Brunei, Vietnam, Thailand, Cambodia, China, Hong Kong, Papua New Guinea, Pakistan, Uzbekistan and Bahrain.

In 2011, the Thai government announced plans to liberalise the Thai financial services sector to encourage financial services firms from the ASEAN+3 countries to establish operations in Thailand, which should encourage more cross-border financial services expansion by Asian banks.

India's largest banks are also expanding internationally, led by ICICI Bank and State Bank of India, which are building their Asian and Middle East branch networks.

The Asian wealth management industry

One of the most important strategic trends transforming Asian financial services is the rapidly rising wealth management market in Asia. This is a key factor that is helping to drive the growth of assets under management in the Asia-Pacific financial centres, and helping to create rapid growth in Asian financial system assets that can be used for expanding lending activities.

While the estimated size of the Asian wealth management industry varies according to different estimates, a report prepared by Swiss financial services firm Julius Baer in 2011, entitled the 'Julius Baer Wealth Report', estimated that the total number of high net worth individuals in Asia in 2010 was around 1.16 million, with wealth of USD 5.6 trillion. According to the report, total Asian HNWI wealth is forecast to triple to USD 15.8 trillion by 2015, of which USD 8.8 trillion will be attributable to Chinese HNWI. According to another report by Merrill Lynch Global Wealth Management and Capgemini, entitled the 'World Wealth Report', the total number of HNWI in the Asia-Pacific reached 3.3 million in 2010, with USD 10.8 trillion under management. Japan is the biggest HNWI market according to their report, accounting for 52.5 per cent of the total number of Asia-Pacific HNWI, while China accounts for a further 16.1 per cent.

The wealth that is accumulating in Asia due to the rapid growth of business empires is also reflected in the estimates of the total number of 'Centa' millionaires, or those with assets of over USD 100 million. According to 'The World Wealth Report 2012' published by Knight Frank LLP in conjunction with Citi Private Bank, there were an estimated 18,000 Centa millionaires in East Asia in 2011, which was greater than the total number of Centas in North America, which was estimated at around 17,000, or in

Europe, where the number of Centas was estimated at 14,000. By 2016, the total number of Centas is forecast to rise to 26,000 in East Asia, compared with 21,000 in North America and 15,000 in Europe. This projection implies significant new wealth creation in Asia amongst the entrepreneurial classes, which will also be reflected in the rise of many Asian businesses.

While the range of the estimates of Asia-Pacific wealth are quite wide, nevertheless they indicate the magnitude of the wealth already in the Asia-Pacific, as well as pointing to the very rapid growth projected over the medium- to long-term. This will be a key driver of the Asian financial services industry, creating strong growth in the asset management industry as well as creating a fast-growing asset base for Asia-Pacific banks to increase their domestic and international lending activities. While US and European banks will also be significant competitors for this business, the strong growth projected across many Asia-Pacific economies in total assets under management will be a significant factor supporting the growth of Asia's own banks as well, particularly in Japan and China, where foreign banks have a limited share of the domestic market.

Asia's fund management industry

The rapid projected growth in financial wealth and the size of total assets under management in the Asia-Pacific region is also resulting in rapid growth in the Asia-Pacific fund management industry. Total fund management assets in the Asia-Pacific at the end of 2011 were estimated at USD 1.5 trillion, according to the data published in the *Financial Times* (27th February 2012, FTfm *Quarterly Industry Review*).

Table 4.2 Asia-Pacific leading fund management markets compared with European leaders

Asia-Pacific	USD billion	Europe	Euro billion
Japan	368	UK	671
China	321	Germany	427
Australia	261	France	268
South Korea	135	Italy	248
India	104	Switzerland	222

Source: *Financial Times* from Lipper Fundfile estimates, FTfm *Quarterly Industry Review*, 27th February 2012.

China – a typhoon in international finance

One of the key structural changes transforming the shape of the global financial services industry is the rise of China. There is a typhoon coming in international finance as Chinese banks internationalise, backed by their large balance sheets. China is forecast to become the world's biggest economy in terms of GDP within a decade, and its large banks are already very big players in the global league of banks when ranked according to assets. There are already six Chinese banks in the global top fifty ranks of the world's largest banks according to size of total assets.

Chinese banks have until recently been very much domestically focused, particularly as the Chinese banking industry underwent a difficult reform process during 2000–07 to reduce the high level of bad debts through major recapitalisation initiatives. However, there have been significant steps taken in the last five years towards greater international operations.

A milestone was the stake taken by ICBC when it acquired a 20 per cent share in South Africa's Standard Bank in 2007 for USD 5.5 billion, which was an important step in developing a more international focus. In August 2011, ICBC also announced that it would acquire an 80 per cent stake in Standard Bank Argentina, the eleventh biggest bank in Argentina ranked by deposits. ICBC has also opened branches in five ASEAN countries and has established a SE Asia RMB processing centre in Singapore. In Indonesia, ICBC has a 97.83 per cent stake in PT Bank ICBC Indonesia, with twelve branches in Jakarta, Surabaya and Bandung, and in Thailand, ICBC acquired a small Thai bank, ACL Bank, in 2010. ICBC announced in early 2011 that it plans to acquire an 80 per cent stake in Bank of East Asia USA to enter the US market.

Table 4.3   Chinese banks: global ranking by assets

Chinese Bank	Global Ranking of Banks by Assets	Total Assets (USD billion)
ICBC	11	1,726
China Construction Bank	18	1,409
Agricultural Bank of China	20	1,301
Bank of China	22	1,281
China Development Bank	36	665
Bank of Communications	50	485

Source: *Global Finance Magazine*, 2010 Ranking of Top Fifty Global Banks.

Similarly, Bank of China, China's most internationalised bank in terms of overseas assets, has developed a large international network of branches and is increasing its global branch network rapidly, particularly in Asia.

As the Chinese economy continues to grow, driving further growth in Chinese bank balance sheets over the next decade, a substantial further expansion is likely to take place in Chinese bank operations globally. This will be underpinned by rapid growth in Chinese trade with the rest of the world, the growth of Chinese investment flows into other countries as well as the growing use of renminbi as the settlement currency for international trade with China.

Eventually, as China becomes the world's largest economy, the Chinese renminbi will in due course become an internationally convertible currency. This will become a key factor supporting the rise of Shanghai, Shenzhen and Beijing beyond their current role as large domestic financial centres for their own domestic economy, and will accelerate their emergence as international financial hubs for the global economy.

In the meantime, Hong Kong's role as the key international financial centre and banking gateway for mainland China will continue, buoyed by the size of the mainland Chinese economy.

Singapore: A leading international financial centre

Singapore's rise as an international financial centre has been very rapid during the last decade. In 2000, Singapore was a significant commercial banking and trade finance centre, but lived in the shadow of Hong Kong. However, in just a decade, Singapore has become one of the world's key international financial centres, closely rivalling Hong Kong.

What brought about this transformation was the characteristic vision of the Singapore government in identifying financial services as a key strategic industry for the future of the Singapore economy. The government carefully developed the suitable regulatory infrastructure to support the development of Singapore as a wealth management and asset management hub. This has encouraged global wealth management and asset management firms to establish their operations in Singapore, to tap the rapidly growing financial assets of the wealthy throughout the Asian region.

Total assets under management in the Singapore financial centre are estimated to have reached SGD 1.4 trillion by
2010, which is equivalent to over USD 1 trillion, based on the
Singapore Asset Management Industry Survey results. Over the
period 2006–10, which also included the peak years of the global financial crisis during 2008–09, the Singapore assets under
management grew at an average annual pace of around 16 per
cent per year.

The success of the Singapore financial centre has been built on
a careful strategy of creating competitive advantage in financial
services as well as clusters of excellence. The Singapore financial
services cluster has been built around excellent financial regulatory and supervision standards by the Monetary Authority of
Singapore, which is a recognised world leader in best practice
standards. The Singapore government has also taken a very strategic approach to creating an attractive environment for various
key segments of the financial services industry to use Singapore as
a key headquarter hub for the Asia-Pacific.

As the financial services cluster in Singapore has continued
to grow, with retail banks, investment banks, asset management
firms, as well as the world's leading legal and accounting firms to
support the financial centre, the Singapore financial services cluster has rapidly grown to become one of the top five international
financial centres worldwide.

With its strategic positioning for the ASEAN, North Asian as
well as South Asian markets, the Singapore financial centre is well
positioned to continue to grow rapidly, tapping the fast-growing
regional demand for international financial services.

Malaysia's ascent as an Islamic financial centre

Within the last decade, Malaysia has become the leading hub for
the Islamic finance industry worldwide, overtaking major financial
centres in the Middle East. This achievement has not only helped
to catalyse the growth of Malaysia's financial services industry, but
has become an important showcase for the rest of the Malaysian
economy of how Malaysia can be a global leader in a knowledge-
intensive industry.

In 2010, Malaysian Prime Minister Najib Razak set out a vision
and road map for Malaysia to become globally competitive in high
value-adding industries. The Islamic finance industry was an

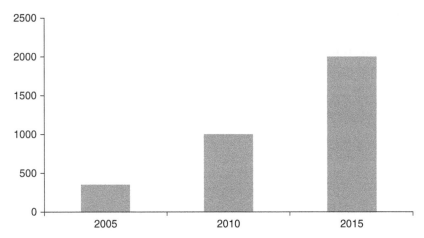

Figure 4.2 Global Islamic assets under management, USD million
Source: Industry estimates.

important part of the strategy for the overall development of the financial services industry, which comprised an important strategic segment of Malaysia's Economic Transformation Programme launched in 2010.

In 2010, Malaysia's Islamic finance industry accounted for an estimated 8 per cent of global Islamic banking assets. The Malaysian government set out an objective under its strategic plan to increase this share to 13 per cent of global Islamic assets under management by 2020, with annual growth in assets under management of around 12–15 per cent per year projected over the decade to 2020.

The origins of Malaysia's Islamic finance industry

In late 2010, when I met with Dr. Zeti Akhtar Aziz, the Governor of Bank Negara Malaysia, she casually mentioned in passing that the first Islamic financial institution in Malaysia was actually founded by her father, Royal Professor Ungku Aziz. This was a remarkable revelation for me, given the instrumental role that Dr. Zeti has played in transforming the Malaysian financial services industry from the rubble of the East Asian crisis into a very competitive, well-regulated financial sector that is now competing in other markets globally, including in other ASEAN countries as well as the Middle East.

The origins of Malaysia's first Islamic finance institution were driven by a need to help poor rural Muslim communities to fulfil the Fifth Tenet of Islam to perform the hajj. Poor farmers with little financial means were often previously obliged to sell their meagre assets, such as livestock or small properties, in order to raise sufficient money for their holy pilgrimage.

Royal Professor Ungku Aziz Ungku Abdul Hamid wrote a paper in 1959 proposing a plan to form a fund to assist the rural poor with funding their pilgrimage. The paper resulted in the creation of the Pilgrimage Fund Management Board in 1969. The Board was restructured in 1995 and renamed Lemaga Tabung Haji.

It is a remarkable achievement indeed for both father and daughter to have played such a key role in building the Malaysian Islamic finance industry from nothing in 1969 and transforming it into the world's leading Islamic finance hub in just four decades.

Drivers of competitive advantage for Malaysian financial services

The success of the Malaysian Islamic financial services centre reflects a number of key factors.

The first and most critical has been the substantial achievements made by the Malaysian government, led by the central bank, Bank Negara Malaysia, together with the securities regulator, the Securities Commission, in reforming and restructuring the Malaysian financial services industry after the East Asian financial crisis. The consolidation of the Malaysian banking industry that took place in 2000 was a key step towards creating a stronger, more resilient financial system in Malaysia.

The second key driver that has been critical for building the competitiveness of Malaysia's financial services industry has been the sustained strategic initiatives undertaken by the central bank and securities regulator to strengthen regulatory standards and corporate governance in the financial system, as well as improving risk management practices. These reforms have been critical in pushing Malaysia's financial services industry towards global best practice standards, creating a competitive environment for the growth of an international financial centre for both conventional as well as Islamic financial services.

Thirdly, the development of Malaysia's Financial Sector Masterplan (FSMP), launched in 2001, created a vision and road map for the process of structural change and transformation of the Malaysian financial services industry, with clear objectives and timelines against which progress could be measured. The effective implementation of this Masterplan has also been a fundamental driver of building competitiveness.

Fourthly, the Islamic financial services industry has also been developed with careful strategic planning and vision, in a structured way. Following the establishment of Tabung Haji, the next major phase of the development of the Islamic finance industry was to permit Malaysia's conventional banks to offer Islamic products and services, allowing them to use their existing infrastructure and balance sheets to support the development of their Islamic financial services. Only after banks had time to develop these Islamic products and services was a dual banking system created, whereby firewalls were put in place between conventional and Islamic banking funds.

A very important fifth step was the creation of an Islamic capital market in the 1990s. The development of the sukuk market in Malaysia has become a key platform of Malaysia's global competitiveness as an Islamic financial centre, with the Malaysian sukuk market accounting for 50 per cent of the Malaysian bond market, which is one of Asia's largest bond markets, with capitalisation of around 98 per cent of GDP. The development of the sukuk market has also created important synergies for the Malaysian stock market, with the total value of the sukuk programme listed on Bursa Malaysia at the end of 2010 being around USD 28 billion, with

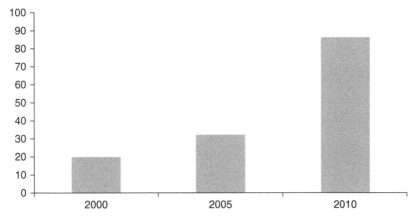

Figure 4.3   Malaysia: Islamic assets in the financial system, USD billion
Source: Bank Negara Malaysia.

Table 4.4 Islamic financial centres
competitiveness review 2010

Country	Overall Rank
Malaysia	1
UAE	2
Bahrain	3
Saudi Arabia	4
Kuwait	5

Source: Kuwait Finance House Research.

one-third of global sukuk issuance in 2010 being listed on Bursa Malaysia.

Sixthly, the Malaysian government has taken a strategic approach to creating a sound and transparent regulatory structure for Islamic finance, as well as building education and training standards for the Islamic financial services industry. Malaysia has emerged as a global leader in developing education standards for the industry, notably through the establishment of the International Centre for Education in Islamic Finance (INCEIF), which was set up by Bank Negara Malaysia. INCEIF has been granted university status by the Malaysian Ministry of Higher Education and currently offers a range of qualifications, including the Chartered Islamic Finance Professional qualification.

The Malaysian Islamic finance centre is ranked first among all the world's Islamic finance centres, according to a recent survey undertaken in 2010. Total Islamic banking assets in the Malaysian banking system are estimated at around USD 86 billion in 2010, which is approximately 8.5 per cent of the global size of Islamic assets under management. In terms of the Malaysian domestic banking system, Islamic banking accounts for around 20 per cent of the total Malaysian banking system measured by assets.

The future outlook for Malaysia's Islamic hub

The Islamic financial services industry globally is growing at a rapid pace, with total Islamic assets under management estimated to have reached USD 1 trillion in 2010. Globally, Islamic assets are estimated to be growing at a rate of around 15–20 per cent per year, a pace of growth that has already been sustained over the last decade. If these trends continue over the next decade, the size of Islamic assets under management will grow very significantly, reaching around USD 2 trillion by 2015, creating tremendous opportunities for the various segments of the Islamic financial services industry.

With Malaysia already having established itself as a leading Islamic financial services hub, the prospects for Malaysia to benefit significantly from the future growth of this industry are tremendous. The opportunities extend across a range of sectors, from Islamic banking products and services, to the sukuk capital markets, as well as to takaful insurance and the Islamic fund management industry.

For Malaysia, the Islamic financial services industry has emerged from humble beginnings in 1969, and now stands at the threshold of a golden age in which Malaysia is set to be the leading global hub for Islamic financial services. Malaysian financial institutions have already expanded their operations to Indonesia, which is the world's most populous Muslim country, and they offer considerable long-term opportunities for Islamic financial services.

The future of Asian financial centres

Since the end of the Second World War, international finance for the global economy has been dominated by European and US banks. This has created vulnerabilities in international financing flows for developing countries, due to large fluctuations in net private financing flows. However, the rapid economic growth of developing countries has significantly increased the share of developing economies' GDP in the world economy. This is also driving rapid growth in the size of domestic financial services firms in some of the largest developing countries, and some of the biggest emerging markets' financial services firms are enlarging their international footprint.

As the Chinese economy continues its ascendancy to become the largest economy in the world over the next decade, this will also drive the growth of the Chinese banks. With the large state-owned Chinese banks already amongst the largest in the world when measured by deposits or size of assets, their balance sheets are set to grow substantially further over the next decade. This will give Chinese banks substantial balance sheet capacity to rapidly expand banking operations globally, providing finance for the expansion of their own companies as well as becoming key global banks for the provision of trade finance, infrastructure project finance and development loans in the Asia-Pacific as well as other emerging regions globally.

With the Indian economy also growing rapidly, and set to overtake Japan in terms of size of GDP by 2025, Indian banks are also expected to become very large in terms of their global ranking. Some of the larger Indian banks are also likely to become much more significant players in global banking, as they expand their international finance and retail banking operations worldwide.

Currently, Hong Kong and Singapore have already emerged as the third and fourth ranked international financial centres, according to the ranking of international financial centres undertaken by the last 'Global Financial Centres Index (GFCI)' published in 2010 by the City of London. While Tokyo is also amongst the world's leading financial centres according to this index as well as financial flows data, it still has a strong focus on Japan-related international transactions and financing linked to Japanese corporations. The large domestic financial centres of the Asia-Pacific, such as Shanghai, Mumbai and Jakarta, are still very much domestic in focus. This reflects to a large extent their regulatory environment, with capital controls limiting the ability of their financial institutions to play a significant role in international finance.

However, Asian banks are set to become a significant force for the diversification of international finance over the next two decades. As China continues to drive the shift in the global economy

Table 4.5 Asian financial centres ranking by City of London GFCI7 Index

Financial Centre	Global Ranking
Hong Kong	3
Singapore	4
Tokyo	5
Shenzen	9
Shanghai	11
Beijing	15
Taipei	21
Seoul	28
Osaka	34
Kuala Lumpur	51
Mumbai	58

Source: City of London 'Global Financial Centres Index', City of London and Z/Yen Group, March 2010.

from West to East, Chinese banks will also play an increasingly important role in international finance. This diversification of international finance away from European and US providers towards a more globalised industry is a positive development, increasing international competition and reducing the vulnerability of developing countries to volatility in international financing flows.

The new global landscape of international financial centres will therefore change very substantially compared to today. A key strategic trend will be the ascendancy of Asian financial centres as the size of the Asia-Pacific economies continues to become a larger share of the global economy.

The rise of Asian MNCs as global corporate leaders and the rise of Asian banks will have many synergies, as has been the case with the growth of Japanese MNCs and their Japanese banking partners. In a similar way, large MNCs from China will provide substantial international banking business to the large Chinese banks as the MNCs become increasingly international in their operations. The same pattern is likely to occur with other emerging Asian economies, including India, Indonesia and Malaysia, which have well-developed banking systems.

Strategic trends for the Asia-Pacific finance industry

A number of key strategic trends taking place in the Asia-Pacific financial services industry will have significant implications for the future shape of the global financial services industry.

Firstly, large Asian domestic banks with rapidly expanding balance sheets will increasingly develop their cross-border activities, initially to provide essential cross-border services to their large domestic MNC clients who are also expanding globally.

Secondly, the largest Asian banks are likely to embark on regional and international growth strategies, involving both organic and M&A-driven expansion. The focus of such expansion will be concentrated on the fast-growing emerging markets of the Asian region as well as other key emerging markets in other developing regions, notably the Middle East and Africa, where trade and investment ties are strongest.

Thirdly, Asian banks will rapidly develop their wealth management and asset management segments, due to the very strong growth in the total size of the middle classes in Asian developing countries. This will be an important driver for rapid growth in total assets under management in the Asian banking industry, creating fast-growing balance sheets for the development of international lending business.

Fourthly, the Asian insurance industry is set for decades of very strong growth. Per capita expenditure on insurance in Asian developing countries remains very low due to relatively low average incomes, but the rapid growth in the size of Asian middle classes will fuel strong growth in this industry.

The key financial centres of Asia will continue to see rapid growth due to the fast-growing economies of the region.

Tokyo will remain one of the world's leading financial centres, barring some natural disaster that causes protracted damage to Tokyo. The Japanese banks and insurance companies are highly sophisticated in terms of their capabilities and offerings, but will need to increasingly look to international markets outside of their traditional comfort zone of domestic Japanese transactions and international lending for Japanese MNCs. This will require considerable repositioning of the internal cultures of Japanese banks and other financial services companies. It is currently far from clear that they will be able to rise to this challenge. If they cannot, then they will face a relatively stagnant domestic market that will limit their future growth potential.

Chinese domestic financial centres will increasingly become leading financial centres by international standards in terms of size and volume of activity, but will not become international financial centres until the yuan becomes a freely convertible currency. Hong Kong will continue to thrive as the main international financial centre for international financial services for mainland China. Shanghai will continue to grow as China's largest domestic financial centre, and its ascendancy will be accelerated by the eventual internationalisation of the renminbi. This will eventually create competition between Shanghai and Hong Kong for the role of China's premier international financial centre. However, this is more of a long-term threat to Hong Kong's financial centre beyond 2020 rather than an imminent problem, since the yuan is not expected to become a fully convertible currency in the near- to medium-term.

Singapore will continue to rise as Asia's leading international financial centre, supported by its strategic positioning as a financial hub for North Asia, ASEAN and South Asia. With many ASEAN economies having relatively underdeveloped financial systems,

Singapore will play a key role as an international financial hub for these economies. The rapid growth of the Asian wealth management industry and total assets under management will also support the rapid future growth of Singapore's wealth management and asset management industry. Singapore will continue to grow in stature as the Asia-Pacific's leading international financial centre, providing investment banking, wealth management, fund management and insurance services to global multinationals in the Asia-Pacific as well as to the rapidly growing high net worth families of the Asia-Pacific region. Singapore's role as a financial centre is also likely to expand far more significantly for capital flows in both directions between the Middle East and Asia. Middle East investment flows will increasingly be allocated towards Asian asset classes rather than in the slow-growing economies of the OECD.

Malaysia's financial centre will also continue to thrive, supported by the regional expansion of its largest commercial banking giants, as well as the rapid growth in its Islamic financial services centre for domestic business as well as for the Islamic financial services markets of Indonesia, South Asia and the Middle East.

As large Asian financial institutions increasingly shift from being domestic players to becoming regional and global players, the need for some form of regional financial architecture in Asia will become increasingly pressing. Therefore the creation of an Asian Monetary Fund, as originally proposed by Japan in 1997, should be an increasingly important strategic priority for Asian financial sector policy-makers in finance ministries and central banks. This will provide a forum for regional regulators from central banks and other financial services regulatory bodies to undertake a wide range of essential roles, including crisis prevention, regional financial sector surveillance, as well as acting in cases of crisis resolution. Importantly, it will also provide a regional forum to help Asian developing countries with underdeveloped financial systems with a wide range of assistance, including policy support, technical advice and training. The case in favour of the creation of an Asian Monetary Fund has become increasingly compelling.

Chapter 5

China

Rising superpower or coming collapse?

China has laid down her three-step strategy towards modernisation. From now to the year 2020, China will complete the building of a comfortable society in an all-round way. By 2049, the year the People's Republic will celebrate its centenary, we will have reached the level of a medium-developed country. We have no illusions but believe that on our way forward, we shall encounter many difficulties foreseeable and unpredictable and face all kinds of tough challenges. We cannot afford to lose such a sense of crisis.

Speech by Chinese Premier Wen Jiabao at Harvard University,
10th December 2003.

China's rise as an economic power

When I first visited Beijing in the early 1990s, my impressions were of a grey, drab industrial city teeming with poverty-stricken beggars seeking alms from foreign visitors. The historic great commercial cities of Shanghai and Guangzhou were rather derelict shadows of their former heyday as commercial and financial hubs, with rotting edifices of beautiful but long-neglected colonial-style buildings from the early part of the 20th century.

Just twenty years later, in 2012, Beijing and Shanghai have been transformed and are virtually unrecognisable compared to their urban landscapes just two decades ago. Beijing is now a modern city with stunning high-rise architecture, beautiful office buildings and brand-new highways everywhere, albeit heavily congested with new model automobiles from the world's major automakers, with plenty of BMWs and Audis in evidence. Indeed, China has become the world's largest auto market, with Chinese domestic auto sales having overtaken the US in 2010 and expected to grow significantly larger over the next decade.

The citizens of Beijing generally look comfortably off, and there is hardly any evidence of people begging anymore. White collar office workers are fashionably dressed, and there are luxury shopping malls everywhere, filled with the outlets of the world's leading brands of clothing, watches and fashion accessories. The Beijing people themselves are warm and helpful, and usually very courteous, although like in any big Asian metropolis, there are also a fair share of fraudsters and rip-off merchants willing to take gullible foreigners for a ride.

On the hour-long drive from Beijing to Tianjin, one of China's major ports and a fast-growing industrial city, the multi-lane highway is brand-new and well landscaped. It is hard to recognise any difference between the infrastructure standards in this Beijing–Tianjin corridor and in Europe. Many of the world's largest manufacturing multinationals have factories and plants in Tianjin, including an Airbus plant with an assembly line for A320 passenger jet aircraft for the fast-growing Chinese civil aviation industry. The scale of urban construction and development underway in Tianjin is immense, with a seemingly endless panorama of apartment buildings and office parks under construction or newly completed.

Shanghai has become a thriving global city, with the major Pudong redevelopment now a futuristic hub for global finance and trade. Shanghai is once again a global metropolis, full of international business travellers and brashly competing with Hong Kong, with the ambition of becoming China's leading financial centre.

The transformation of China from a socialist industrial society in the early 1990s to a global economic leader is also reflected in the large numbers of foreign workers from the OECD countries who have flocked to China to find their fortune or to at least gain experience in the world's rising economic power.

As Japan in the 1980s and 1990s was a magnet for Western youth, so China has become the new beacon for ambitious school-leavers and graduates from Europe, North America and Australia. They realise that the economic gravity of the world economy is shifting towards Asia with China at its core, and that experience of doing business in China as well as Chinese language skills will be important attributes in the future. The European economic crisis and soaring unemployment rates for youth in the European Union are only accelerating this trend.

The importance of China as a trade and investment partner has also risen very considerably during the last decade, particularly in the Asia-Pacific region. China has become the largest export market for a number of Asia-Pacific countries, including

South Korea, Australia, Malaysia and Thailand. Its importance in the trade rankings for other Asian countries has also risen very substantially.

I was recently a speaker on a conference panel together with Jim Rogers, one of the world's greatest investment gurus, who now lives in Asia. He told the audience that his children are learning Chinese in school, which he believes will be an important competitive advantage for them in their careers as China's economy continues to rise. That demonstrates the strength of his conviction in the continued future economic ascendancy of China.

However, China's future economic ascendancy is not preordained. History is replete with examples of the rise and fall of great powers. It is not necessary to go far back in the history books to find such cases. Some of the most spectacular economic collapses have been in the relatively recent past. The bursting of the Japanese economic bubble in the 1990s ended its post-war ascent and destroyed its ambitions of becoming the world's largest economy. The collapse of the Soviet Union created a period of political and economic turmoil within the former USSR. This ended the Cold War, propelling the world into a new era with a single global superpower, the US.

> China has much to lose. It is not a democracy, and there is no established routine for changing governments. Failure to achieve a satisfactory growth rate – generally defined as eight per cent – could easily lead to political turmoil, and political turmoil in China would be disastrous for the world. (George Soros, 'The Crash of 2008 and What It Means')

Is the Chinese economic miracle facing collapse?

For over three decades since economic liberalisation commenced in 1978, China has sustained average annual GDP growth rates of around 10 per cent per year. Since the commencement of economic liberalisation and reform policies in 1978 under Senior Leader Deng Xiaoping, the per capita GDP of China in US dollars at nominal prices has risen from USD 228 per year in 1978 (United Nations data) to USD 5,400 by 2011.

This has resulted in tremendous progress in human development. According to World Bank poverty measures, the proportion of Chinese living in extreme poverty has declined from 84 per cent in 1981 to just 13 per cent by 2008. The World Bank has estimated that around 662 million Chinese people have been lifted out of extreme poverty since 1981.

However, as China's economic ascent has continued, there has been ongoing scepticism and cynicism about its ability to sustain this momentum. Many books and articles have been written in the last ten years or so about the forthcoming collapse of the Chinese economy, presumably with regular reprints as the year of impending collapse has moved further into the future. There must have been some good careers made in being a persistent prophet of doom for China over the past couple of decades.

I have found that the highest level of anxiety about the future of China has come from business executives and economists in Western Europe and the US, who have a deep conviction that the Chinese single-party state is inherently unstable and that eventually this will trigger political turmoil and collapse. The recent fall from political grace of Bo Xilai, one of China's most well-known political figures, has again triggered renewed fear in the US and Europe about political instability in China.

While these risks from an inflexible, single-party political system are very real and cannot be dismissed, concerns in the Asia-Pacific about the risks of imminent political turmoil and upheaval in China seem to be considerably less acute than in Europe and in North America.

Ironically, some European senior business executives and economists were so focused on the risks from a political and economic collapse in China in the years leading up to the global financial crisis of 2008–09 that they failed to notice the risks building up in their own backyard in Europe. When the US was engulfed by the US subprime debt crisis, European financial houses and economies were also plunged into crisis due to mounting financial losses amongst many of the largest European banks.

The EU crisis became greatly enlarged soon afterwards, as rising sovereign debt levels resulting from rescue efforts following the global financial crisis triggered political turmoil and deep recessions in a number of the EU member countries. Instead of China collapsing it was Europe that collapsed, in a political and economic maelstrom. The ultimate irony was that China's own economic rebound, triggered by fiscal and monetary stimulus measures, contributed a large part of the global economic recovery momentum that led the world economy out of recession in 2010.

However, political risks in China do remain a key concern over the medium- to long-term outlook, due to the continuation of a one-party state with little sign of significant political reforms. The threat of social instability remains one of the main policy concerns of the Chinese government. China already faces sporadic outbreaks of civil unrest and anti-government protests in several regions, including Tibet and Zhejiang. Each year, there are also thousands of incidents of social unrest at local level, for a wide spectrum of disparate reasons which range from industrial unrest due to working conditions and discontent over wages, to protests about land rights and environmental issues.

For the Chinese top leadership, the threat of political unrest is seen as a key risk to the Chinese economy. During the Arab Spring in 2011, the Chinese government significantly increased its policing in inner city areas to ensure that similar popular protests did not commence in Chinese cities. The perceived risk of political unrest has been mitigated so long as strong economic growth has created large net new employment each year. However, should the Chinese economy enter a period of weaker economic growth, there are risks that discontent and popular protests could escalate if there are large and rising numbers of unemployed workers unable to find new job opportunities.

The risk of social unrest is also high due to the large share of the Chinese population that still lives close to the poverty line.

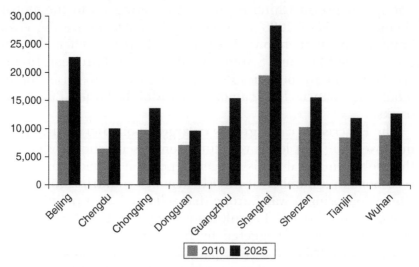

Figure 5.1   Chinese megacities: population to 2025, thousands
Source: UN, World Urbanisation Prospects, 2011.

Although there have been very substantial achievements in poverty reduction since 1978, the World Bank estimates that vulnerability to poverty remains high in China, with around one-third of the Chinese population re-entering poverty around once every three years due to various forms of income shocks related to issues such as volatile agricultural production or disruption of industrial employment.

The Chinese government therefore attaches a high strategic priority in its economic planning, ensuring a relatively stable economic growth performance and avoiding boom-bust cycles. After the global financial crisis, the Chinese government undertook large-scale fiscal stimulus measures to boost infrastructure investment in order to ensure that the Chinese economy did not slide into recession as a result of the severe shock to the export sector caused by deep recessions in the US, Europe and Japan. Substantial credit expansion through the state-owned banks was also undertaken, with a 50 per cent expansion in credit during 2009–10.

However, these measures, albeit having substantial positive impact on economic activity in the near-term, created risks of increased economic imbalances in the Chinese economy as the rapid expansion of new lending by the banking sector created risks that, over the medium-term, significant bad loan exposures will eventually need to be realised as a result of the rapid and indiscriminate lending practices during the 2009–10 credit boom.

There is also considerable concern amongst financial sector analysts about the quality of the large-scale lending to local governments during 2009–10 to fund a vast array of new projects. Much of this lending is expected to eventually end up as non-performing loans, and this creates additional risks of deteriorating non-performing loan ratios in the banking sector.

The Chinese banking sector was significantly recapitalised between 2000 and 2007 after a previous episode of very high bad debts, with new capital raised through the private sector by part-privatisation, including the sale of stakes in Chinese banks to foreign institutional investors. The Chinese Ministry of Finance has announced in April 2012 that Chinese banks will need to hold higher capital reserves, as it takes steps to ensure banks are preparing adequately for the expected surge in non-performing loans that need to be written off over the medium-term.

The risks from a banking sector crisis are very severe to the overall economy, as countless past banking crises worldwide have demonstrated, notably in Japan after the bursting of the economic bubble in the 1990s and in the US and Europe during the global financial crisis of 2008–09. However, the capital adequacy ratios of Chinese banks have improved significantly since their recapitalisation, with the risk-weighted capital adequacy ratio of the Chinese banking sector having risen from an annual average of −2.3 per cent during 2000–04 to +11.8 per cent by 2011.

The Chinese government also had to grapple with the consequences of the credit boom in the property sector in 2010–11, with rapid growth in property prices forcing the government to significantly tighten credit flows for the property sector in order to curb speculative investment and the rising risks of a property bubble building. Tighter liquidity conditions and falling demand for new properties in the large Chinese cities has taken its toll on Chinese real estate companies, with property development firms now also facing increasing liquidity problems, heightening the risks of financial collapses amongst some property developers.

It is the conjunction of such economic problems in key sectors of the economy such as construction and banking that could create the conditions for a hard landing for the Chinese economy, particularly if the global economy is also going through another recession or very weak growth. A protracted hard landing in China could then result in the deterioration of economic conditions that could trigger greater social unrest and the potential to lead to political turmoil.

In the near-term to medium-term, the risks of such political upheaval are still limited due to the ability of the Chinese government to use economic policy levers to stimulate economic growth. The government debt to GDP ratio is still relatively low, at around 25 per cent of GDP, and moderate at around 50 per cent of GDP even after allowing for potential contingent liabilities related to local government borrowings. Therefore, the national government can still use fiscal stimulus if GDP growth slows.

Furthermore, a key national policy priority continues to be the reduction of social and economic inequalities between the relatively richer coastal provinces and the inland western provinces. China's period of rapid economic growth since 1978 was strongly driven by rapid export growth and significant foreign direct investment inflows into the manufacturing sector. Much of this export- and investment-led growth was concentrated in the coastal provinces of China, particularly in the Pearl River delta and Yangtze River delta regions. This reflected the competitiveness of these regions in terms of logistics, since key raw materials such as iron ore and coal could easily be shipped in to these coastal areas, while the finished export goods could equally easily be shipped out to export markets.

The rapid growth of coastal China had created significant disparities in household incomes as well as economic infrastructure between coastal Chinese provinces and inland western provinces. Fearing the potential scope for such widening inequality to trigger social unrest, the Chinese government embarked on a massive programme of infrastructure development and urbanisation in the western provinces, which accelerated during the 2009–10 period as a significant portion of fiscal stimulus measures were directed towards infrastructure development of western provinces.

Therefore in the event that significant fiscal policy stimulus is needed to prevent a hard landing in China, there are still considerable economic development objectives to be met in the western provinces in order to continue the development of modern physical infrastructure as well as accelerate urban development.

Consequently the Chinese government still has the capacity to use fiscal stimulus measures to avert a hard landing scenario over the near- to medium-term, should this be necessary. However, the risks would increase considerably in case of a protracted global recession, as it would strain even the fiscal resources of China to continue to pump-prime the economy for a number of years. Therefore the risk of political turmoil associated with a hard landing in the Chinese economy, while still a low probability, is an important downside risk scenario that becomes increasingly high impact with each passing year due to the rising importance of China to the global economy.

Can China's economic ascent be sustained?

For the last three decades China has achieved an annual average real GDP growth rate of around 10 per cent. This has transformed China from a very poor developing nation into a lower middle income country within one generation. For a nation with a population of 1.2 billion, this is an incredible achievement.

During the next decade and beyond, China's economic growth rate will moderate significantly due to two key driving forces. The first is the impact of demographic ageing on China's population, which will result in a significant slowdown in the size of youth cohorts entering the labour force over the next three decades. This will be a gradual process, but will have an increasingly significant impact in the decade leading up to 2030 and is expected to reduce China's potential growth rate, since labour is a key factor of production.

The second driving force which will result in some moderation of China's economic growth rate is the declining marginal productivity of capital. China has invested heavily in new capital, with strong growth in infrastructure development for decades, and this has generated significant gains in productivity. However, the returns on future large-scale capital investment for uses such as infrastructure development would be more limited, as the marginal productivity gains from additional investment in infrastructure diminish.

The combination of these two factors will play a significant role in a moderation in Chinese growth momentum by 2020, with average annual GDP growth expected to slow down to the 7–8 per cent growth rate range, slowing further to an average 6–7 per cent GDP growth by 2030.

During the last three decades when China was growing at such a rapid pace and average annual economic growth was 10 per cent, many economists used to define a hard landing for the Chinese economy as GDP growth slowing to below 6 per cent. Indeed, that is still the line in the sand often used as a guide to define what a hard landing is.

However, in the next decade and beyond, the dynamics of the Chinese economy will change significantly, albeit at a gradual pace, due to the impact of demographic ageing and the declining marginal productivity of capital. Gradually, the potential growth rate of the Chinese economy will adjust downwards over time, and the definition of what constitutes a hard landing for the Chinese economy will also need to adjust downwards.

Therefore by 2020, growth moderation to between 6 and 7 per cent will no longer be perceived as automatically signalling a collapse in the Chinese economy into a hard landing scenario. By 2030, as the potential growth rate moderates further, annual GDP growth of around 5 to 6 per cent will probably be close to the potential GDP growth rate for the Chinese economy. However, by 2030, the moderation of Chinese economic growth to what would seem to be such pedestrian rates compared to the recent past should not ring alarm bells that the Chinese economy is slumping into a hard landing.

A key concern related to a hard landing for the Chinese economy is that it would significantly increase unemployment rates and that the economy would be unable to generate sufficient new jobs for new entrants into the workforce. This would increase the political risk that such circumstances could create the tinder for social unrest. However, as China's demographic ageing will reduce the number of new entrants into the workforce over the next two decades, the annual average GDP growth rate required to deliver the necessary volume of new jobs for the workforce will also gradually be lower, requiring a redefining of the line in the sand that is a 'China hard landing'.

Therefore, the definition of what constitutes a hard landing or severe slowdown of the Chinese economy needs to gradually adjust downwards in the next two decades. No country can be expected to grow at a 10 per cent average annual rate indefinitely. When other East Asian tiger economies such as Japan, South Korea and Singapore were in their stages of rapid industrialisation, they also achieved very strong average annual growth rates that later moderated as their economies matured. China will go through a similar process.

The Chinese government itself has indicated this in its '12th Five Year Plan', and has set a GDP growth target for the 2011–15 period of 7.5 per cent real GDP growth per year. The '12th Five Year Plan' is a transition towards a more balanced economic growth path, with less emphasis on rapid economic growth and greater priority given to rebalancing economic growth away from an export- and investment-driven growth model towards higher domestic consumption.

Other key objectives include a greater focus on sustainable economic growth, with increasing attention on environmental policies to improve the quality of growth. This includes a shift towards greater use of renewable energy such as solar power, as well as significantly improving usage of clean coal technologies in coal-fired power stations to reduce carbon dioxide and sulphur dioxide emissions. The use of natural gas for electricity generation is also growing rapidly.

Nevertheless, the shift down in growth gears by the Chinese government does not fundamentally alter the underlying picture about the economic ascendancy of China. Based on GDP growth of around 7 to 8 per cent per year, China is still expected to overtake the US to become the world's largest economy by 2020. With average GDP per capita in China already at over USD

5,000, continued average annual growth of over 7 per cent per year over the next decade will still deliver significant further gains in per capita income. Key strategic trends such as the growing global importance of Chinese consumer spending and the rise of Chinese multinationals will continue to alter the global economic landscape even if China is growing at 7 to 8 per cent per year instead of 10 per cent per year.

This does not imply that China is somehow immune from a hard landing altogether. As former Federal Reserve Chairman Alan Greenspan often stated, 'the business cycle has not been repealed'. Therefore, China will have recessions in the future. The growth rate that constitutes a recession for China will change though. Instead of 6 per cent GDP growth being a hard landing, the growth rate that is considered the boundary below which the economy is slipping into recession will gradually be adjusted downwards. Eventually, the standard global definitions of recession, such as two quarters of negative real growth, may even become applicable to China. However, this process will likely take some decades, as Chinese average economic growth rates drop below 5 per cent per year.

Moreover, as China ascends to the position of becoming the world's largest economy by around 2020, a Chinese recession will become a far greater shock to the world economy than in the past, with major negative transmission effects through trade, investment and financial markets channels to the rest of the world.

China's economic reform agenda

Despite the tremendous economic successes achieved by China since 1978, there are still significant national economic challenges that are at the forefront of government priorities.

One of the most important policy priorities for the '12th Five Year Plan' for the period 2011–15 is to rebalance the economy away from its traditional growth engines of investment and exports, which have been the key drivers of economic growth since 1978. A vulnerability created as a consequence of this dependence on investment and exports has been that the structure of the Chinese economy has altered significantly since the 1970s, with the share of private consumption having declined substantially. The importance of this vulnerability became clearly evident during the global financial crisis in 2008–09, as global demand for

Chinese exports slumped, resulting in millions of export sector workers losing their jobs while the key export growth engine went into sharp reverse, putting the Chinese economy into a nose dive which was only stopped by massive fiscal and monetary policy stimulus measures.

Meanwhile, the economic imbalances in the overall structure of the Chinese economy persist. Household consumption as a share of GDP has declined from around 55 per cent of GDP in the early 1980s to around 33 per cent of GDP by 2011. This is a very low share of total GDP compared with other large developed and developing economies, and this has made China too dependent on investment- and export-led growth.

However, with per capita GDP now exceeding USD 5,400 and set to rise significantly further over the next decade, the Chinese savings rate as a share of total income should gradually decline, allowing a greater share of total income to be spent on consumption. This is a pattern that has also occurred in other Asian industrial economies, such as Japan and South Korea.

Some rebalancing of the economy towards increased consumption as a share of GDP is therefore likely to occur over the next two decades, albeit gradually. This will also have significant implications for China's external account imbalances. While Chinese economic growth was driven by exports and investment as key growth engines, the rapid growth in exports resulted in large and growing trade surpluses. Successive US administrations and the US Congress have been extremely vociferous in their criticism of China's undervalued currency, on the grounds that it is giving Chinese exporters an unfair competitive advantage and has resulted in substantial US job losses over several decades.

China's burgeoning foreign exchange reserves and large bilateral trade surpluses are seen as clear evidence by the US Congress that China has been pursuing this strategy of maintaining an undervalued exchange rate. However, if Chinese domestic demand does gradually rise as a share of GDP over the medium-term, this is likely to result in a decline in the size of the Chinese current account surplus as a share of GDP, reducing one of the key pillars of support for sustained strong renminbi appreciation.

Indeed, there have already been some initial signs that this is taking place, with the Chinese current account surplus as a share of GDP declining from 10.1 per cent of GDP in 2007 to just 2.7 per cent of GDP in 2011. This is not just a result of a fast-growing GDP denominator either. In nominal USD terms, the Chinese trade surplus halved from USD 300 billion in 2008 to USD 155 billion in 2011.

The Chinese government and People's Bank of China have, therefore, already begun signalling that the room for further renminbi appreciation may be very limited, at least in the near-term. While the IMF still expects China to have a substantial current account surplus over the medium-term, in the order of 4 to 4.5 per cent of GDP by 2017, this is subject to significant uncertainty given the current account surplus had already fallen to below 3 per cent of GDP in 2011, with a further narrowing expected in 2012 as the Eurozone slumped back into recession, hitting Chinese exports to the EU.

The flying geese

The Chinese economy is also facing another major transformation over the next fifteen years due to the impact of rising labour costs in coastal China. A number of factors are contributing to this rise.

Firstly, as rapid growth in western Chinese provinces has resulted in a tightening supply of migrant workers for the labour supply pool of coastal Chinese factories, this has helped to drive up wage pressures.

Secondly, the Chinese economy is facing a long-term trend of ageing demographics, partly a reflection of China's one child policy, and this is also progressively reducing the size of new cohorts of workers entering the labour force each year.

Thirdly, the marginal productivity of capital is gradually declining as China has invested heavily in modern infrastructure and equipment, making it progressively more difficult to deliver rapid productivity growth on additional capital investment. This means that strong wages growth can no longer be easily offset by strong productivity growth, which has the effect of pushing up the annual average rate of unit labour cost rises.

As a result, coastal Chinese provinces which had become the factory of the world for low-cost manufacturing such as textiles and clothing as well as consumer electrical and electronic goods will now face a gradual erosion of labour cost competitiveness over the next fifteen to twenty years. This is the same 'hollowing out' of manufacturing industry that was faced by Japan, South Korea, Hong Kong, Singapore and Taiwan in the past, as they progressively lost their low-cost manufacturing industrial base as their wage costs made them uncompetitive in these segments of industry.

The 'flying geese' model of industrial development, a theory originally developed by Kaname Akamatsu, is therefore likely to apply to China's next stages of industrial development. The 'flying geese' model proposes a theory of industrial competitive advantage whereby countries start with low-cost manufacturing industries then gradually progress up the value-adding chain. This pattern has already been evident in the evolution of manufacturing industry distribution in East Asia since the 1960s.

However, due to the immense size of China in terms of its labour market and geography, the structure of the Chinese labour market is far less homogenous than some of the other industrialised countries of East Asia. While coastal China is already seeing its competitiveness in low-cost manufacturing eroded, other Chinese provinces that are further inland still have considerably lower wage costs than the coastal provinces where the manufacturing industry is currently agglomerated.

Therefore, the 'flying geese' pattern that occurs in China may be a somewhat different variation of what has happened in other East Asian countries. While firms that are engaged in low-cost manufacturing may decide that coastal China is increasingly uncompetitive for their segments of production, they may be able to establish factories elsewhere in China, where labour costs are still relatively low.

Of course, this will also depend on the transport logistics involved, and moving far inland may not be feasible for firms that require close access to coastal ports for large volumes of imported inputs or for large-scale export volumes. However, with the domestic Chinese consumer market growing rapidly, the structure of Chinese manufacturing is also gradually shifting towards a greater focus on end use domestic markets, and for many segments of manufacturing, moving further inland may still be a feasible option.

The 'hollowing out' of coastal China is likely to take place in two main geographic directions.

Firstly, a considerable segment of low-cost manufacturing that is displaced out of coastal China will remain in China, located in western inland provinces with lower manufacturing wage costs.

Secondly, some of the 'hollowing out' of low-cost manufacturing will be displaced to other low-cost competitor nations in Asia, notably in ASEAN. ASEAN countries with low wage costs are likely

to be significant beneficiaries of the 'hollowing out' of China.
The countries that are relatively well placed to compete for such
low-cost manufacturing operations are Cambodia, Vietnam and
Indonesia. Depending on the progress of political and economic
reforms, Myanmar could also eventually emerge as a destination
for low-cost manufacturing.

Some manufacturing segments with medium-cost manufacturing operations may also decide to move to Thailand and Malaysia,
due to the relatively good infrastructure and relatively good business climate compared to Cambodia, Vietnam and Indonesia.
Thailand is ranked 17th in terms of ease of doing business according to the World Bank 2012 ranking, and Malaysia is ranked 18th.
In contrast, Indonesia is ranked 100th. Of course, ASEAN will not
have a monopoly on the 'flying geese' leaving China. Bangladesh
has already emerged as an alternative preferred location to China
for low-cost textiles and clothing manufacturing.

Meanwhile China's manufacturing industry in the coastal provinces will need to undergo a significant restructuring away from
low-cost manufacturing towards higher value-adding segments of
manufacturing. The service sector is also likely to experience rapid
growth, as rising household incomes drive consumer demand for
services such as banking, insurance, retail trade, communications,
health services and tourism.

China as a rising superpower

Even with a gradual moderation of China's potential growth rate,
it is still expected to become the world's largest economy by 2025.
The relative size of its economy will continue to increase by 2030,
as the total size of its GDP surpasses the US and EU to an even
greater extent.

The geopolitical and economic implications of China's rise are
already evident and far-reaching.

Firstly, the importance of China as a key trade and investment
partner will continue to grow, particularly for Asia-Pacific nations.
China seems set to become the largest export market for almost
all Asia-Pacific economies, and for some nations, this is already
the case. Similarly, China will become increasingly important as
a source of both foreign direct investment and portfolio capital
flows for most Asia-Pacific countries, as its economy becomes the
world's largest.

Secondly, the role of Chinese corporations in the global economy will continue to increase, supported by the Chinese government's own policy of encouraging large Chinese multinationals to internationalise. This will make large Chinese multinationals more significant global competitors in international markets, with a strong push for expansion in their hinterland of East Asia.

Thirdly, the rise of China to become the world's largest economy will also be accompanied by rising Chinese consumer demand, as the burgeoning Chinese middle class creates a wave of consumer spending that will form the new engine for global consumer spending growth. The implications are wide-ranging. For commodities, the implications are for continued strong growth in demand for energy, including oil, natural gas, coal and new renewable energy sources such as solar and wind energy. Rising incomes and the growing size of the middle class will also drive demand for agricultural commodities, including grains and soya bean, as well as meat, dairy products and fisheries products. Much of this rising Chinese demand for soft commodities will need to be met by imports, which will create significant growth in demand for international supplies of such soft commodities for the Chinese market. This could be a very positive long-term trend for agricultural exporting nations, such as the US, Australia, New Zealand, Brazil and some sub-Saharan agricultural exporters.

The development patterns of other East Asian countries such as Japan and South Korea also imply that the intensity of use of metals will still rise further in China for some years, albeit eventually declining again. The implications of these trends are that China will still have a seemingly insatiable thirst for commodities for years to come, albeit subject to the volatility of the business cycle. From a strategic perspective, that means that energy security will be a central focus of Chinese strategic policy, with implications for its political and defence policy settings.

Fourthly, Chinese financial institutions will become increasingly international, with banks expanding their international operations both to support their own corporate sector but also to play a bigger role in global finance.

Fifthly, China will gradually play a much more central role in global geopolitics. As it becomes the world's largest economy, its economic weight in international policy-making bodies such as the G20, IMF, World Bank and Asian Development Bank will continue to grow in importance. With its ever-expanding trade and investment ties with nations worldwide, its ability to project its foreign policy objectives with the cooperation of other sovereign states will become far more effective, giving it increasing geopolitical influence.

It is the sixth dimension of China's superpower status that is the most uncertain and that has the potential to create a more unstable geopolitical global order. As China's economy grows to become the world's largest, this will inevitably lead to rising defence spending and increasing military capability. As China's GDP increases and eventually overtakes the US, the size of Chinese GDP as a share of total Asian GDP, which is already one-third, will increase further.

This implies that among the Asia-Pacific nations, China's military capability will become significantly larger than that of any other Asian nation, including Japan and India. With China's technological capability also rising rapidly, the future use of military power as an extension of Chinese foreign policy could become a key risk to regional peace and security. Whether this will actually happen is uncertain. However, given China remains a one-party state and will have a rising military capability, other Asian countries are increasingly concerned about the potential for the growing asymmetry in Asian military power to become a source of geopolitical instability in the Asia-Pacific. How this will play out in regional geopolitical terms will depend on the foreign policy and defence policy of future Chinese governments.

Chapter 6

Can India eclipse China?

In the democracy that I have envisaged, a democracy established by
non-violence, there will be equal freedom for all. Everybody will be his own
master.... Once you realise this you will forget the differences between the
Hindus and Muslims and think of yourselves as Indians only ...
Mahatma Gandhi, Public speech at All India Congress Committee,
Bombay, August 1942

Living in China's shadow

In 2011, India's per capita GDP was around USD 1,400. This compared with Chinese per capita GDP of USD 5,400. Yet in the 1950s,
both countries were among the poorest and least developed, with
largely agrarian societies engaged in subsistence farming. Even by
the time Senior Leader Deng Xiaoping's economic reforms commenced in China in 1978, there was little difference in per capita
GDP levels and living standards between the two nations.

How did China manage to move so far ahead of India since
1978, so that the average per capita GDP level in China became
almost four times higher than that of India?

There were a number of ingredients to China's very successful economic performance after the process of liberalisation
commenced.

Firstly, the Chinese reforms rapidly moved towards a policy of
attracting foreign direct investment into low-cost manufacturing,
with the creation of special economic zones to attract foreign multinationals to establish low-cost manufacturing hubs for export.

Secondly, the Chinese began to compete for low-cost manufacturing at a time when rising labour costs in Japan were already
affecting the competitiveness of low value-adding segments of
Japanese industry, so China was able to tap into the growing
stream of relocation of factories out of Japan. Other Northeast
Asian economies also faced 'hollowing out' of their manufacturing
sectors, including Hong Kong and Taiwan.

Therefore by using a development model that focused on investment and exports, China was able to rapidly build up its role as a low-cost location for global export processes, attracting large inflows of foreign direct investment.

India was much slower to embrace market liberalisation and economic reforms than China. After independence in 1947, the Nehru government had moved in the direction of creating a socialist economic model, based on the development of domestic heavy industries such as steel, aluminium and chemicals, with the use of heavy tariff barriers to protect domestic industries from foreign competition.

Even after China had moved in the direction of economic liberalisation, India remained enchanted with its socialist model, although it was failing miserably to deliver sufficient economic growth to provide much more than marginal annual improvements in living standards.

For the first three decades after independence, India made only slow progress towards poverty reduction, and on the eve of its first significant steps towards liberalisation in 1991, the estimated share of the total population living in extreme poverty was 51 per cent.

The good

The beginning of India's economic liberalisation process began in 1991, after a balance of payments crisis forced political changes. The election of Narasimha Rao as Prime Minister resulted in the selection of Manmohan Singh, a former central bank governor, as Finance Minister. With the economy in crisis, there was a pressing need for economic reforms, and this made Manmohan Singh's political task of undertaking widespread reforms easier.

A wide range of reforms were undertaken to open up the economy, including streamlining project approval processes, sweeping reductions in tariffs, allowing foreign direct investment, including providing for automatic approval processes for a number of industries.

Financial sector reforms were also made, allowing foreign institutional investors to invest in the domestic stock market.

Although the pace of these liberalisation measures was relatively slow, these represented the most significant economic reforms in India since independence. As the reform measures continued to be gradually implemented, the Indian economy began to show some moderate improvement in underlying growth. One industry sector that benefited quite substantially from these reforms was the automotive sector. Prior to the 1991 reforms, there were two main makes of car on the road: One was the Premier Padmini, known as the 'Fiat', since it was based on the Fiat 1200 GranLuce Berlina, a Fiat design that had originally been introduced to the Italian auto market in 1957, and the other was the Ambassador car, a 1950s Morris Oxford model, which had been produced in Britain in the late 1950s, and was being manufactured under licence in India. With the local auto manufacturers protected from foreign competition, they were able to charge considerably higher margins for their autos. The sight of Indian roads being filled by these antique models until the 1990s became an object of ridicule about the Indian economy. What is more, due to the lack of competition, there were long waiting lists to get delivery of these cars. I recall my father having to wait many months for the delivery of the new Fiat car he had ordered.

However, after the reduction of tariff barriers and the opening up of the automotive sector, the Indian auto industry began to gradually attract foreign manufacturers. The auto sector began to grow at a much more rapid rate as the capacity constraints of the old regime had been removed.

Total automotive production in India has expanded very considerably since 1991. Total vehicle production reached around 3.5 million units by 2010, including both passenger vehicles and commercial vehicles, compared with just 800,000 units in 2000.

Most importantly, India has actually become an international auto manufacturing hub, and has even begun to export cars. Instead of just two antiquated models of cars on the road, the Indian roads are filled with a wide range of international as well as domestic auto models, with many of the world's largest automotive manufacturers having established auto production facilities in India.

India has also become a leading producer of two-wheelers, mainly of motorbikes and scooters, with total production of two-wheelers reaching 7.5 million by 2009, of which 1 million were exported.

Korean auto manufacturer Hyundai began production in India in 1996; soon after the liberalisation measures for the automotive sector began to be implemented. Hyundai has built up its Indian production capacity considerably since that time, and has become India's second largest auto manufacturer with annual production reaching 600,000 units. Hyundai has built up its exports to become the largest auto exporter out of India, with India now the leading global hub for Hyundai for the manufacture of compact cars. Hyundai has also invested in a major auto R&D facility in Hyderabad.

India's own auto producers are also becoming competitive global players since the liberalisation of the automotive sector. Tata Motors has become India's largest vehicle manufacturer, leading production of commercial vehicles and being the third-largest producer of passenger vehicles. Tata Motors has also undertaken an ambitious mergers and acquisitions programme to build up its global footprint and technological capability.

In 2004, Tata Motors bought Daewoo's truck manufacturing division, and in 2008 it bought Britain's iconic Jaguar Land Rover from Ford for USD 2.3 billion.

This case study of the automobile industry reflects the tremendous impact that economic reforms have made in improving the competitiveness of India's manufacturing sector. The auto sector is estimated to have become one of the largest contributors to the manufacturing sector. From a situation just over twenty years ago where India's auto industry was heavily protected and producing only two antiquated models, it has become a dynamic automotive industry which is also rapidly becoming a major auto exporting hub.

Despite the remarkable transformation of India's auto sector, which is creating substantial multiplier effects in the development of India's manufacturing sector, the real catalyst for the more dynamic performance of the Indian economy has been the information technology industry.

Information technology services and business process outsourcing have grown from an estimated 1.2 per cent of Indian GDP in 1998 to around 7 per cent of GDP by 2011. The industry generated around USD 88 billion of revenue in 2011, of which USD 59 billion were from exports and a further USD 29 billion were related to domestic sales. The remarkable growth of the IT export sector has driven up its importance in total exports from a share of around 4 per cent in 1998 to around 25 per cent by 2011.

While the IT sector has become a key contributor to both exports and GDP, and now accounts for around a total of 2.5 million jobs in the Indian economy directly, as well as 8.3 million jobs through indirect multiplier effects, the importance of the IT sector has gone far beyond this. It has served as a benchmark of

Indian excellence, creating greater confidence in the Indian corporate sector about the ability of Indian firms to compete globally and aim for best practice global standards.

The strength of corporate India has grown significantly in the last decade, with rapidly growing ranks of large industrial firms across many sectors of the economy, ranging from heavy industries, such as steel and chemicals, to construction and infrastructure development. Similar progress has been achieved in the service sector, with large Indian private sector firms across a wide range of service industries, including communications, financial services, hotels and transportation.

The depth and range of the Indian corporate sector has become one of the key strengths of the Indian economy, creating an important growth driver for economic development.

The bad

Although the Indian industry has made substantial progress since the beginning of economic liberalisation in 1991, India still lags far behind China in terms of basic measures of economic performance, such as total size of GDP and per capita GDP. Given both countries have roughly similar population sizes, the comparison is striking. According to World Bank estimates of global poverty levels, the share of the population living in extreme poverty had declined to 13 per cent of the total population of China in 2008, compared with 32.7 per cent of India's total population.

The reasons why India has not matched China's growth performance can be attributed to a number of factors.

One of the great limiting factors constraining the Indian economic performance is the size of the public sector debt, which is around 75 per cent of GDP. India has run such high government debt levels for many years, despite relatively strong GDP growth since 2003. The inability of the Indian government to translate rapid economic growth into sustained fiscal consolidation has been a key weakness in macroeconomic policy which is increasingly creating economic vulnerability. With such high government debt levels, a large share of India's budget expenditure is eaten up by the debt service payments. While India's debt is domestically funded, which mitigates the macroeconomic vulnerability to international capital markets, this has, nevertheless, been a key constraint to the Indian economy.

This is particularly the case because India's infrastructure has lagged far behind that of China, and this is where the different fiscal profiles of the two countries have been extremely adverse for India. Whereas China has kept its national government debt level relatively moderate, at around 25 per cent of GDP, and runs fiscal deficits that are also very moderate as a share of GDP, India's government debt as a share of GDP is triple that of China, while the fiscal deficits it has been running are also extremely high, ranging from 8 to 10 per cent of GDP each year over the past decade, after taking into account fuel and fertiliser subsidies as well as state government debt.

With such high government debt levels and fiscal deficits, India's public sector has very limited capacity to fund infrastructure development from the public purse compared with China. While the Indian government has tried to increase public sector investment in infrastructure, this is very difficult to do when the government is also trying to pursue medium-term fiscal consolidation.

Therefore, India has been forced to put far greater reliance on private sector infrastructure funding through mechanisms such as public-private partnerships. While this has been delivering good results, India faces a massive infrastructure deficit across many sectors of the economy, notably in power generating capacity, but also in roads, rail, ports and many other segments of infrastructure.

This has a direct negative impact on the potential growth rate of the Indian economy, reducing India's annual potential GDP growth rate by at least 1 per cent. Furthermore, such infrastructure deficiencies also increase supply bottlenecks at times of rapid economic growth, which also increases inflationary pressures in the economy and forces a tighter monetary policy stance than would otherwise be the case.

One sector where lack of adequate infrastructure investment has clearly been a major problem is agriculture, with supply-side bottlenecks regularly driving food prices up sharply, which creates spikes in the inflation rate. While factors such as weather cannot be entirely mitigated by infrastructure investment, weak infrastructure does play an important role in contributing to these problems, for example, the lack of adequate water storage and irrigation systems makes it to cope with poor rainfall. India's lack of adequate food storage and distribution infrastructure also results in very high food loss rates, with an estimated 25 to 30 per cent of the fresh fruit and vegetable crop lost due to inadequate storage and distribution infrastructure. Lack of sufficient good quality storage capacity for grain stocks is a key source of vulnerability for Indian food security.

These are pressing problems that are directly reducing India's annual GDP growth rate by a considerable margin; however the government has been unable to make significant progress on these issues despite having achieved a number of consecutive years of strong economic growth of around 8 to 9 per cent.

While the Manmohan Singh Congress-led coalition government has increased its policy focus on India's 'soft power' as a foreign policy tool, particularly trying to capitalise on the global affection for India's Bollywood movies, there needs to be far more focus on 'hard power', especially the electric kind that turns on lightbulbs and drives industrial machinery.

There is a desperate need for ramping up electricity generation capacity rapidly. In 2011, India's installed electricity generation capacity was 200 Gigawatts, the fifth-largest generating capacity in the world. That may sound impressive until I tell you that China's installed electricity generating capacity at the end of 2011 was 1,050 Gigawatts, more than five times greater than India's. In 2011, 300 million Indians still had no access to electricity. The problems of the Indian electric grid and lack of adequate generating capacity were highlighted in July 2012, when massive power outages hit the Indian grid system. During this blackout, an estimated 600 million people in northern India faced an extended power blackout, disrupting transportation networks, commerce and households.

During India's 11th Five Year Plan that ended in the 2011–2012 fiscal year, India added 55 Gigawatts of additional power generating capacity, which far surpassed the achievements of previous Five Year Plans. Indeed, the additional capacity added in the 11th Five Year Plan was approximately equal to that of the previous fifteen years, so there has been significant acceleration of power infrastructure development. Moreover, the Indian government has targeted adding a further 76 Gigawatts during the 12th Five Year Plan that ends in 2017.

Despite these efforts, the lack of sufficient power generation capacity is a major disrupting factor to the growth and development of India's economy, notably for the manufacturing sector, which needs to grow at a rapid pace to provide long-term jobs growth for India's fast-growing workforce. If the Indian government cannot get its act together on infrastructure development, Indians will be left singing and dancing their favourite Bollywood songs by candlelight while emerging economies in North-east Asia and ASEAN continue their rapid economic development. So much for Indian 'soft power'.

The ugly

While poor economic management and bureaucratic red tape are certainly well-known weaknesses of the Indian system of government, another great problem that is particularly severe is corruption. While it is impossible to accurately measure the exact amount of government revenue that is eroded by corruption, anecdotal observations by high-level officials who have a good understanding of the extent of the corruption problem indicate very high figures indeed.

The figures that are often mentioned are far greater than 20 per cent of total government revenue, which indicates the scale of the problem. Given India's fiscal difficulties, such high attrition rates are a major constraint on the ability of the government to deliver essential services and to provide public infrastructure.

After decades of public cynicism about government corruption, the frustrations of the ordinary masses were vented in widespread protests against corruption during 2011–12. The protest movements have galvanised around the leadership of a social activist, Anna Hazare, who has led the peaceful protests against corruption.

In some parts of India, extremely high poverty levels and anger about the inequalities of land ownership have also fuelled significant violence through the Naxalite rebels, who have considerable control in some regions of India. The Indian Prime Minister Manmohan Singh has identified the Naxalite rebel movement as one of the most significant threats to Indian security, with the government unable to regain control of some regions where the Naxalites are deeply embedded.

While military responses have had mixed success in suppressing the Naxalites, the fundamental root causes that provide succour to the Naxalite cause will not be effectively addressed until rapid economic development and improvement living standards in the worst-affected regions erode support for the Naxalites.

India's demographic challenge

According to United Nations Department of Economic and Social Affairs' recent population projections done in 2010, India will overtake China to have the world's largest population by 2021. The UN population projections estimate that India's population will reach 1,401 million persons in that year, compared with 1,241 million in 2011. By 2030, India's population will rise considerably further, reaching 1,523 million.

So long as India can continue to generate annual average GDP growth of over 6 per cent per year, India's rising population will continue to create opportunities for business, due to the fast-growing demand for a wide range of products and services that it will generate. However, it also creates vast challenges for policymakers, as they grapple with the economic and social needs of India's burgeoning population.

This is not a new phenomenon. At the time of independence in 1947, India's population was just 350 million, so the Indian government has already had to cope with the challenges of a 900 million increase in India's total population since independence. Nevertheless, the scale of the task is still immense.

A key structural trend will be the continued urbanisation of India, as the size of Indian cities continues to rise rapidly. By 2025, there will be 55 Indian cities with a population exceeding 1 million persons, according to United Nations forecasts

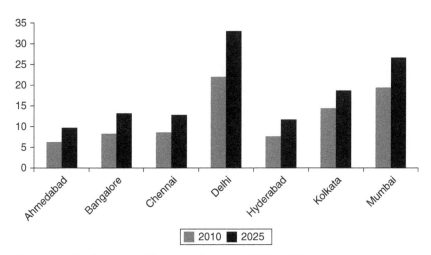

Figure 6.1 Indian megacities: population to 2025, millions
Source: UN, World Urbanisation Prospects, 2011.

of population growth in urban centres. Of these, there will be seven Indian megacities, with populations of around 10 million or more.

The rapid growth in population in India's cities will create ongoing challenges for government authorities to plan urban centres using best international practice. Governments will need to provide adequate physical infrastructure to cope with the rapidly growing population, as well as to have a strong focus on economic development initiatives to create employment for the rapidly growing urban population. Building smart cities that are energy efficient will also be an important factor for India, given the existing problems with the inadequate energy infrastructure. Use of smart grid technology will be a key priority in this process. The importance of smart grid technology for India's future cities is reflected in the decision by Crompton Greaves Limited, India's leading power equipment manufacturer owned by a Indian conglomerate the Avantha Group, to acquire Spain's ZIV Group, a smart grid automation firm, for USD 185 million in 2012.

Major projects are already underway in India to develop smart cities, with Lavasa smart city, close to Pune, being developed by Indian property conglomerate Hindustan Construction Co. Limited, with IT technology being provided by Indian IT multinational Wipro together with US IT giant Cisco.

In Kochi, close to Cochin International Airport, SmartCity Kochi is being developed in a joint venture between the Government of Kerala and Dubai's Tecom Investments, which has invested in the development of smart cities in other parts of the world, including Dubai and Malta.

In an example of pan-Asian private sector co-operation for Indian urban development, Singapore's Ascendas through its Ascendas India Development Trust together with Japan's Mizuho Corporate Bank and JGC Corporation have signed a Memorandum of Understanding with the Government of Tamil Nadu to build a world-class integrated township in Chennai.

Therefore although India's rapid urbanisation will create large infrastructure challenges for the Indian government, it will also create vast opportunities for both Indian and international construction and infrastructure companies for decades ahead. This could transform India's urban landscape, creating smart cities, modern office parks and urban residential developments designed to be competitive for the knowledge economy of the future.

Future India

Although India has shown a strong growth performance during the last decade, fears have again emerged among international investors that India could slip back to a weaker pace of economic growth for a protracted period. The resurgence of India's old economic woes of large twin deficits on both fiscal and current accounts have contributed to these fears, creating persistent selling pressure on the Indian rupee. This has forced significant intervention in international foreign exchange markets by the Reserve Bank of India during 2011–12, in an effort to stem the sharp falls in the rupee. However, as this also eroded foreign exchange reserves, it has created new anxieties about India's external account vulnerabilities.

However, there are a number of reasons for optimism about the Indian economic outlook beyond the cyclical pressures of the business cycle.

Firstly, unlike China, India's demographic profile remains youthful for decades ahead. While this also puts pressure on the policy-makers to deliver an economic performance that will generate sufficient new jobs to employ the future cohorts of youth entering the workforce, it does also create a favourable structural dynamic in the economy.

Secondly, the Indian corporate sector is no longer the same creature that it was twenty years ago. Protectionist barriers have been torn down in large segments of the economy, and there is considerable strategic focus in India's large corporates to compete globally and establish international business footprints. This is evident in the strategies of many of India's largest multinationals, ranging from the IT industry to automobiles and pharmaceuticals. Therefore, the Indian corporate sector is becoming increasingly dynamic and internationalised, and is a catalyst for positive change in the Indian economy. There is tremendous talent and vitality in the Indian corporate sector, both at the level of the large companies, and amongst the burgeoning ranks of India's fast-growing medium enterprises. Adam Smith's 'invisible hand' is alive and well in India, creating a strong underpinning for long-term growth in the Indian corporate sector.

Thirdly, there are signs of greater investment flows into Indian infrastructure. While these are in no way comparable to China's infrastructure development in the last decade, nevertheless it does represent significant change in the Indian infrastructure landscape. India's largest international airports have been redeveloped or rebuilt with the infusion of private sector capital, with brand-new airports having been completed in Hyderabad and Bangalore. A second phase of airport redevelopment in the second tier cities is now underway.

There has also been progress in the construction of new toll roads as well as some port developments. Private sector investment into port development will be critical to improving port infrastructure, and developments such as the privately owned Adani Mundra Port have created advanced port and related infrastructure that is critical for Indian trade development. Similarly plans by India's Reliance Power Ltd. and Kakinada Seaports together with Royal Dutch Shell PLC to build a 5 million ton per year LNG terminal in the state of Andhra Pradesh will be important for the future development of India's electricity generating capacity. These improvements in infrastructure will deliver important productivity gains for the Indian economy, albeit not to the extent of China.

Fourthly, India does not have the same economic imbalances as China. China has been growing very rapidly based on the dual growth engines of exports and investment. India does not have the same dependency, with consumption as a share of GDP being very high, at 68.7 per cent of GDP in 2010. This is approximately double the ratio in China.

Therefore, the structure of the Indian economy is very favourable for the rapid growth of consumer demand. Research by the Asian Development Bank in its report 'Key Indicators for Asia and the Pacific 2010' estimates that the size of the Indian middle class has grown by around 205 million persons since 1990. This equates to an annual increase in the size of the Indian middle class by around 20 million persons per year.

This creates a powerful dynamic for an economy in which consumption accounts for almost 70 per cent of GDP. Whereas China is struggling to tap the spending power of its consumers due to the low share of private consumption in total GDP, India is very well positioned to see the rising spending power of the consumer classes translate into more rapid growth in demand for domestic goods and services.

India has gradually liberalised its foreign investment regime and opened up a significant share of industry to foreign investment, and these have triggered a very substantial uptrend in foreign direct investment flows into India. Prior to the commencement of economic liberalisation in 1991, foreign direct investment into India was a trickle compared to that into China. At the outset of economic liberalisation, total FDI inflows into India in 1991–92 was just USD 129 million, according to Reserve Bank of India statistics, an amount that would seem modest for even a small frontier market economy, let alone Asia's second BRIC.

By 2004–05, FDI into India had risen to USD 4.7 billion, which was still a negligible amount for a BRIC economy and a mere fraction of FDI into China. However, just three years later, FDI into India had soared to USD 34.8 billion, and since then annual FDI has not fallen below this level. In the 2011–12 financial year, FDI flows reached USD 46.8 billion, a record high.

To a large extent, this reflects the attractiveness of India's fast-growing domestic consumer market for global multinationals. The importance of large emerging markets for the global revenue growth strategy of multinationals has increased significantly since the global financial crisis in 2008–09, and this has made India even more important to the core growth strategy of multinationals in a wide range of industry sectors. Despite the economic woes of India portrayed in media headlines during late 2011 and during 2012, Coca-Cola announced in June 2012 a long-term investment plan for an additional USD 5 billion of investment into India by 2020, while IKEA also announced plans in the same month to invest around USD 2 billion into India and open 25 stores in major cities across the country.

When considering the long-term growth outlook for China versus India, it is also important to consider that China will have two major drag factors on its future long-term growth rate. The first drag factor is the ageing demographic profile of China. This means that future cohorts of youth entering the workforce will be steadily declining in numbers, which will put pressure on wages in China as well as creating potential shortages of low-cost labour. India does not have this problem over the next three decades.

The second drag factor affecting the outlook for Chinese economic growth rates is that the marginal productivity of capital will be declining. China invested heavily in infrastructure and technology in the last two decades, and this delivered strong productivity growth rates for industry. However, the marginal productivity of incremental investments of capital will eventually decline, as the quality of China's stock of capital is already high. Ironically, due to the woefully inadequate investment in infrastructure in India since independence, the declining marginal productivity of capital is not a problem India will face in the foreseeable future. Indeed the situation is quite the opposite, as the marginal productivity of incremental investments in India will be high for many years to come, due to the chronic shortages of investment in capital.

The implications of these two drag factors are that Chinese GDP growth rates over the next three decades will moderate significantly. Whereas Chinese GDP grew at an annual average rate of 10 per cent per year in the last three decades, the Chinese government has estimated an annual average GDP growth target of 7.5 per cent per year for the '12th Five Year Plan' which runs from 2011–15. This is closer in line with what the potential growth rate of the Chinese economy is over the next decade.

Furthermore, China's potential GDP growth rate will moderate further by 2030, and will probably be closer to around 6 per cent than the historic annual average of 10 per cent.

With India's annual average GDP growth rate having the potential to be 8 per cent per year or possibly even slightly higher over the next two decades, India's growth performance may start to gradually outshine that of China.

However, the relative size of the Indian economy compared with China will still be considerably smaller, due to the GDP gap that has emerged since China embarked on its economic reforms. Therefore from a geopolitical standpoint, although India will be a rising economic power in the Asia-Pacific, and will overtake Japan in terms of total size of GDP in around a decade, it will not be able to significantly close the GDP gap with China within the next thirty years.

Nevertheless the role of India as an ascendant economic power will be one of the most significant global trends after the rise of China, as it will provide the second major growth engine for the Asia-Pacific region, driving rapid growth in trade and investment with many Asian countries, notably Japan, China and ASEAN.

India's future growth trajectory could improve significantly with better governance and greater mobilisation of essential infrastructure investment. These changes could further enhance India's potential growth rate and the potential GDP growth rate could move higher as a result.

After China, India will also be an important driving force for commodities markets, as the rapid growth in the size of the middle class will drive demand for key mineral and agricultural commodities.

Barring an extreme failure of government or a swing in economic policy away from liberalisation and economic reforms, India seems to have sufficient growth drivers to maintain potential GDP growth rates of 7 to 8 per cent over the next three decades.

If the government undertakes a gradual process of fiscal consolidation, this could further boost the potential growth rate by reducing government fiscal deficits and allowing more rapid public sector infrastructure investment. This would boost productivity growth and potential GDP growth. India should be able to achieve an additional 1 per cent boost to long-run potential GDP growth through sustained fiscal consolidation, eventually allowing increased public sector and public–private partnership infrastructure investment, which would push the Indian long-run potential GDP growth rate into the 8–9 per cent range.

As in the great Indian literary epic, the Ramayana, that is so central to Hinduism and Indian culture, India is currently facing a tremendous battle between the forces of good and evil. In the Ramayana, Rama and Lakshmana, the heroic figures representing courage and virtue, fight the forces of evil, epitomised by Ravana, the demon king. Whether India can find leaders who will fight the many-headed and divisive forces of evil, including corruption, poverty and religious chisms, will be crucial in determining the future economic development path of the nation. National leadership focused on good governance, and tapping India's very strong talent pool of technocrats, could significantly accelerate India's long-term growth path.

Chapter 7

Japan

The next Greece?

Everything is a dream.
Man's ambition is but a dream of dreams.
With my thoughts on grand Osaka
I must vanish like the morning dew.
Hideyoshi Toyotomi, Imperial Regent of Japan, written before his death in 1598.

The next Greece?

In March 2012, a former senior official of the Japanese Ministry of Finance, Takatoshi Ito, who was Japan's Deputy Vice Finance Minister for International Affairs from 1999 until 2001, gave an interview in which he warned that Japan could eventually end up going down the same road of sovereign debt crisis as Greece.

The key trigger, he said, would be when local financial markets in Japan are no longer able to finance Japan's new debt issuance, forcing the government to either tap global financial markets or have the Japanese central bank, the Bank of Japan, purchase the new debt issuance, effectively printing money.

One of the key factors that has significantly reduced the vulnerability of Japan to such high levels of government debt is that over 90 per cent of the total Japanese sovereign debt has been held by domestic Japanese investors, including Japanese banks, insurance companies, pension funds and corporate treasuries, as well as retail investors.

According to recent Bank of Japan figures, foreign ownership of Japanese government bonds accounted for around 8.5 per cent of the total stock of Japanese government bonds by the end of 2011, which was already a significant rise compared with the end of 2010, when the ratio was at 6.5 per cent.

The Japanese parliament, the Diet, has made the difficult political decision to double the 5 per cent sales tax by 2015, to prevent the fiscal outlook from deteriorating. Still, Japan will increasingly have to look to global capital markets to fund its sovereign debt. As Japanese reliance on international capital markets for sovereign debt financing rises, the risks start to increase that Japanese bond yields will move higher. However, with the debt to GDP ratio already over 200 per cent of GDP in gross terms, if bond yields rise as a result of the need for foreign funding, this could trigger an escalating crisis.

For over a decade now, Japan has been able to fund its sovereign debt at very low interest rates, with ten-year government bond yields having been in a range of between 1 per cent and 2 per cent. Therefore, the Japanese government is extremely vulnerable to any significant increase in bond yields. Even a 1 per cent increase in yields would virtually double the cost of financing, creating a very large increased burden on government fiscal capacity to finance the debt.

Yet just twenty years ago, Japan was a rising economic power with a growing confidence in its economic destiny. The publication of a book in 1979 by Ezra Vogel, a Harvard University professor, called *Japan as Number One: Lessons for America* was given a euphoric reception by the Japanese public, with the Japanese language edition becoming a bestseller in Japan.

Having lived in Japan during the crest of its economic wave, I witnessed at first hand the economic confidence of the Japanese government and corporate sector. There was a strong belief that Japan could actually catch up with the US in terms of total size of GDP, and that Japanese corporations would continue to rise as global leaders in many different sectors. In financial services, for example, a number of Japanese banks were joining the ranks of the world's largest.

I certainly felt a sense of arrogance in the attitudes of many senior officials, reflecting their own economic success and expectation that Japan was heading towards becoming a leading global economic power. In general, I perceived a strong attitude of superiority towards other Asian races, with Japan now a member of the rich group of nations, equal with the Americans and Europeans, while the rest of Asia were regarded as inferior, poor and backward. With hindsight, it was indeed hubris about the Japanese economy. This attitude was most evident amongst many senior government officials and corporate executives, while many other Japanese whom I met in those days in a more social context were much more friendly and engaging.

By the early 1990s, Japan's heyday was already over, although this was not apparent at the time. The Japanese economic miracle of rapid economic growth since the 1960s that had transformed the country from rubble at the end of the Second World War into one of the world's leading economies was about to end rapidly.

Japan's economic bubble burst in 1990 with a property sector and stock market crash that created a protracted banking sector crisis as many large property firms went bankrupt. The problems for the banking sector were magnified because soaring property prices over the past decade had fuelled rapid growth in lending with property as collateral. When property prices collapsed, it created a wave of bad debts as companies that had used inflated property values to back their borrowings were unable to refinance their debts.

The ten years following the bursting of the bubble, from 1991 until 2000, became known as Japan's lost decade or 'Ushinawareta Junen', with little net economic growth achieved over that period. The banking sector took more than a decade to complete its protracted consolidation and deleveraging of bank balance sheets.

The Great Hanshin earthquake of 1995 that destroyed Kobe heaped further woes on Japan amidst its crisis. Although the Japanese government did a fantastic job of post-earthquake reconstruction in Kobe, and created a modern, vibrant city from the ruins, the cost of reconstruction was substantial, at an estimated USD 120 billion. The very modern Kobe Earthquake Memorial Museum, which I visited in 2011, provides a valuable documentation of the disaster and disaster management techniques, albeit quite unhelpful for foreign visitors because most of the explanatory text is only in Japanese. This is downright silly given the large number of foreign visitors to Kobe who are interested in learning about the disaster. For me, the museum was a haunting recollection of the Kobe I had lived in, that had disappeared forever, although the new Kobe that has emerged from the disaster is a vibrant, beautiful city.

With the Japanese economy continuing to face rising competitive pressures from other emerging economies in various areas of low-cost manufacturing, Japan also faced several decades of 'hollowing out' of its manufacturing sector, as low-value segments of manufacturing production were moved by Japanese multinationals to other locations worldwide.

The process of banking sector consolidation was very protracted, but finally over a decade later the banking sector deleveraging process came to an end, and credit expansion gradually turned positive again.

However, the woes of the Japanese economy were hardly over, and the decade from 2001 to 2010 became the second 'lost decade', as the Japanese economy suffered further setbacks, including a deep recession during the global financial crisis of 2008–09, due to the transmission effects of the slump in world trade caused by the banking crises in the US and Europe. Despite economic recovery in 2010 as the world economy rebounded, supported by fiscal stimulus measures, the Japanese economy again entered a mild recession a year later, after the devastating Tohoku earthquake hit the coastline of Northeast Japan with massive destruction and loss of life following devastating tsunamis.

Japan as number three

After two lost decades, the Japanese economy faces enormous economic challenges due to the very high level of government debt as well as the problem of rapidly ageing demographics, which is resulting in Japan's population actually declining each year.

The excitement and euphoric attitudes of 1990 when Japanese government and business felt a sense of destiny that it would become the world's leading nation has been replaced by a mood of persistent negativity as Japan has had to cope with decades of economic difficulties. Instead of aiming to become the world's number one economy, as Japanese had envisaged in the late 1980s, they have now sunk below China in terms of total size of GDP, and have gone downwards in the global league of largest economies to number three. Over the next two decades, the Japanese economy also faces the real prospect of being overtaken by India in terms of total size of GDP, albeit Indian per capita GDP will still be considerably lower than Japan's for the foreseeable future.

The decline of the Japanese economy has brought considerable changes in the attitude of Japanese society and business towards the emerging Asian economies. Even as early as 1997, I was amazed by the humility of a central bank adviser from Japan's central bank, the Bank of Japan, who visited me while I was working as the chief economist of a fund management group. I had expected a fairly haughty attitude from a senior central banker from one of the world's largest economies, but instead I was startled to find that after our discussions had been underway for just a short time, the central banker was virtually wringing his hands as he discussed the economic woes they were confronting. He asked with the greatest of humility for our advice as to how Japan could rescue itself from its crisis. Sadly, we did not have any magic solutions to offer him, and we could only sympathise with him at the challenges the BOJ was facing.

Indeed, soon after that, I and other members of our investment committee at the fund were rather taken aback when our chairman suddenly called us in and said we should sell all the fund's Japanese assets, bringing our Japan exposure down to zero. In the end we did not act as radically, as it would have created substantial risks to our ability to meet our benchmark performance targets for clients, but we certainly were heavily underweight Japan for a long time.

The decline of the Japanese economy and collapse of the stock market bubble resulted in the Nikkei 225 Index falling from its December 1989 peak of 38,916 to a low of 8,605 after the earthquake and tsunami in March 2011.

Even Japan's long-held role as the leading economy in the Asia-Pacific has now been usurped, as China has overtaken Japan in 2010 to become the Asia-Pacific's largest economy. Thus China, as the world's second-largest economy, has pushed Japan into third place in the global ranking, and this has triggered increasing concerns within Japan about the rising economic and military power of China and the implications for Japan in the future.

Moreover, while the gap in size of GDP between China and Japan is still relatively small, China is growing at an annual pace of around 7 to 8 per cent, while Japan is hardly growing at all. Therefore over the next decade, the gap between China and Japan in terms of overall size of GDP will widen very substantially.

Yet some external observers of Japan still have the impression that the nation is doing relatively well, since unemployment is low and the nation still gives the impression of being wealthy, with high living standards. Unfortunately, this is the wrong conclusion. The nation has paid for this economic stability with the large fiscal deficit spending its government has undertaken over the last twenty years, and this has resulted in a huge accumulation of government debt.

When Japan eventually has to confront its government debt problems, this will result in fiscal austerity measures that will bite hard. As the Europeans have recently discovered, there is no free lunch when it comes to sovereign debt. While successive

European governments were able to live on borrowed time by running up government debt, eventually a price has to be paid for this. The EU countries at the heart of the European sovereign debt crisis are finding out the hard way that it is very difficult to manage a smooth exit from such accumulated debt problems.

The inevitable conclusion must be that even in favourable economic circumstances, Japan faces a long path of fiscal consolidation over the next decade, at a time when its economic growth rate is already very weak and the size of the Japanese population is declining.

The key question is whether it is already too late for Japan to avoid a protracted fiscal crisis that will result in the cost of financing government debt rising significantly higher, forcing ugly austerity measures that will plunge an economy that is already barely growing into a extended recession. Is Japan the next Greece?

Rebuilding the Japanese economy

Japanese modern history shows that Japanese society and its business sector are extremely resilient. Rebuilding Japan from the ashes of the Japanese urban landscape after the Second World War into one of the world's most advanced economies was a testament to this.

Therefore despite the tremendous challenges, the efficiency of the Japanese economy and the industrious workforce are important competitive advantages.

However, two crucial elements are needed to stabilise Japan's debt mountain and reduce the risks of a fiscal crisis.

Firstly, as the Japanese government has already clearly identified, there is a need to raise revenues in order to stabilise the fiscal deficit and gradually eliminate the primary deficit. This they have proposed to do by lifting the consumption tax from 5 per cent to 10 per cent, in a staggered process over a number of years. The consumption tax would be raised to 8 per cent by 2014, and then to 10 per cent by 2015. While this is not the full solution on the revenue side, it will be a key element of the strategy to gradually reduce the fiscal deficit. This will already help to boost investor confidence in the outlook for Japanese government debt. Secondly, Japan's potential GDP growth rate needs to improve. As the EU sovereign debt crisis has shown, it is extremely difficult to reduce government spending and raise taxes at a time when the economic growth rate is very low or negative. In such a situation, there is a significant risk that fiscal austerity measures could actually push the economy deeper into recession, which can also result in fiscal revenues declining while social security payments rise due to higher unemployment. Overall, this negative cycle can have the perverse effect of increasing the fiscal deficit rather than reducing it, as well as potentially pushing an economy into recession.

Therefore, lifting Japan's potential growth rate will be a key strategy for gradually reducing government debt levels. There are still avenues available for Japan to continue to pursue reforms that enhance economic competitiveness. Many sectors remain heavily protected, particularly in services. Further liberalisation and deregulation is essential to improve competitiveness. For example, the tendering system for government contracts is still relatively closed to foreign firms, despite decades of negotiations on liberalisation.

The EU Internal Market Commissioner Michel Barnier stated in April 2012 that only 28 per cent of Japanese public tenders are open to EU firms. Further liberalisation of the Japanese domestic market in construction and services will help to improve competition and lower costs.

Apart from deregulation and improving competition in the Japanese domestic markets, Japan also needs to catalyse growth in various key industries by becoming more export-oriented. With the Japanese domestic market projected to show relatively weak growth in the next twenty years, Japanese firms in many service sector industries that have been heavily focused on protected international markets need to look abroad for new markets.

For example, there has been a relative lack of focus on the tremendous opportunities from international tourism. The Japanese Tourism Agency was only established in 2008. There has been little focus on catering to foreign tourists, with major attractions in tourism centres such as Tokyo and Kyoto having very limited English language signs, which makes it very difficult for foreign tourists to fully benefit from the attractions.

International tourist visits to Japan amounted to around 8.6 million visits in 2010, which is considerably lower than to Singapore, which had 11.6 million tourist visits in 2010, and far below that of the UK, which attracted 30 million international tourists in 2010. Japan's overall tourism industry accounts for only around

Table 7.1   Tourism as share of
GDP, 2010

Japan	2.2
Austria	5.4
Switzerland	5.0
New Zealand	4.1
Singapore	4.0
France	3.7

Sources: JTA; national government
sources.

2 per cent of GDP. This is very low compared with other countries such as Austria, Switzerland, the UK and France.

The JTA has the objective of lifting the share of tourism in GDP to 3 per cent by 2016. According to Japanese government estimates, the tourism sector has the potential to contribute 5 per cent of Japanese GDP.

The opportunities for Japan in the international tourism segment are very substantial, given the most rapid growth in global consumer spending over the next twenty years will be from middle-class Asian consumers, from countries such as China, India, Indonesia and Vietnam. China, in particular, offers a huge opportunity, due to the close geographic proximity and the very rapid growth in the total numbers of middle class households in China that can afford international tourism with their new affluence.

However, these tourists from emerging Asia are definitely not going to speak Japanese, so there will need to be a substantial reorientation of the Japanese tourism workforce to be better trained to deal with foreign visitors. Obviously the first priority will be for tourism and hospitality staff to learn English, as tourism staff in many other tourism destinations have done.

Of course, this type of cultural change towards learning English and other major international languages will also be critical to boosting Japan's economic competitiveness in other industries, including sectors such as health care and financial services. For decades, large segments of the Japanese economy have hidden behind protectionist walls as well as having an inward-looking focus, which they were able to get away with while the Japanese consumer market was growing strongly. Those days are over, and many segments of the Japanese economy will need to globalise or die a slow death.

I was delighted to be attending a speech by the eminent Japanese former Vice Minister of Finance, the famous 'Mr Yen', Professor Eisuke Sakakibara, when he made a passionate call for Japan to change its focus away from the Japanese domestic market to major growth markets such as China, India and Indonesia.

> Because of large and deep domestic markets, many Japanese companies – both manufacturing and service companies – have made their first priority the domestic market. Then comes the international market. That needs to be reversed in future. Speech by Professor Eisuke Sakakibara, Professor of Aoyama-Gakuin University, Tokyo at Nomura Asia Equity Forum, June 2012.

Apart from the considerable potential of the tourism sector, there are other industries which have considerable potential for future growth by tapping international markets.

The financial services industry is another sector with potential. During the late 1980s, Japanese banks had begun to expand globally, but after the collapse of the Japanese property and stock market bubble, banks were confronted with a decade of consolidation and they deleveraged their balance sheets. This resulted in many of the Japanese banks withdrawing from international markets to concentrate on their domestic consolidation process.

However, over the last decade, Japanese banks have been relatively unaffected by the global financial crisis. At a time when Asian markets need rapid growth in new trade, finance flows as well as other types of credit, meaning Japanese financial services firms may again have considerable opportunities for expanding their international business activities. The prospects for Japanese firms are assisted further by the significant deleveraging of European bank balance sheets currently underway, which is forcing many European banks to reduce their lending activity in the Asian market.

It is these types of strategic opportunities for repositioning Japanese industries towards global markets that offer considerable potential for boosting Japanese economic growth rates. If the potential growth rate of the Japanese economy can be increased by this new focus on global markets, it could provide a significant boost to the ability of the Japanese government to undertake fiscal consolidation over the medium-term.

Meanwhile, the core export sectors of the Japanese economy, which comprise high value-added manufacturing products such as autos and electronics, have been experiencing 'hollowing out' for decades, as lower value-adding segments of the supply chain are moved to locations in lower-cost manufacturing hubs such as China, India, and Thailand.

The share of manufacturing in Japanese GDP has declined from around 35 per cent in the 1970s to around 18 per cent by 2010. This represents a halving in the contribution of the Japanese manufacturing sector to total Japanese GDP. The total number of manufacturing firms in Japan has fallen by around one-third since 1995, reflecting this substantial reduction in the share of manufacturing in the national economy.

Therefore, Japan faces strong pressure to improve its ability to compete in new export industries, particularly in services, while the traditional manufacturing export industries which were the growth engines for Japan in past decades face increasing cost pressures and 'hollowing out'.

In 2011, Japanese companies spent USD 89 billion on mergers and acquisitions with companies abroad, as they aggressively expanded their global footprint to improve their ability to compete in international markets. A further USD 23 billion was invested in outbound M&A activity by Japanese firms in the first quarter of 2012. This surge in M&A activity reflects an increasing recognition by Japanese firms of the need to expand into international markets, and while many of the largest deals have been done by Japan's biggest global corporations, there are also many smaller to mid-sized firms that are becoming increasingly engaged in building their international markets.

Japan's future engagement with emerging Asia

Japan has several competitive strengths that have made it one of the world's strongest economies and given Japanese households per capita incomes that are among the highest in the world. These strengths include a highly educated and disciplined workforce, technological leadership in many sectors, and a corporate sector that has many of the world's largest and most competitive multinationals.

Therefore, although Japan now faces a very difficult long-term economic outlook due to its very high government debt levels and ageing demographics, it has the underlying competitive economy that creates a strong foundation for the economy to rebound.

However, whether it is able to do so will depend on a number of factors. A key obstacle is political discord and a lack of willingness among a large share of the parliamentary representatives to support reforms. The nation is also characterised by an inward-looking defensiveness that seeks to preserve the homogeneity of Japanese culture.

If Japan is to overcome its economic challenges, it will need to either adapt or suffer a slow decline that could at some point accelerate into a deep fiscal crisis. Unlike 1853, there will be no modern equivalent of Commodore Perry and his 'black ships' to force change upon the Japanese nation.

Therefore, a key public policy priority for Japan will be to focus on new strategic industries where Japan can build up its competitive advantage and engage with fast-growing international markets.

Japan will also need to adapt to the new realities of the changing geopolitical landscape of Asia. The rise of China as a global superpower will create significant changes in political and economic relationships in the region, and will require Japan to work in closer cooperation with regional partners.

Some of the key strategic priorities for Japan's engagement with emerging Asia will include providing a lynchpin for monetary cooperation through the ASEAN+3 Chiang Mai Initiative Multilateralisation and the ASEAN bond fund programmes. However, enhanced bilateral engagement is also required to support Japan's commercial interests to develop new export markets.

Another key priority for Japan will be to have far greater bilateral engagement with India, with strong complementarities between Japan and India in a wide range of industries. For Japan, India provides a rapidly growing consumer market creating new opportunities for a very large range of Japanese products.

For India, Japan offers advanced manufacturing capabilities in a wide range of sophisticated industries, including automobiles, IT hardware and other electronics. One of the greatest obstacles India faces to its economic development is the weakness of its physical infrastructure, such as ports, roads, power and water. In contrast, Japan is one of the most advanced countries in construction technology and engineering, as well as in construction equipment. Therefore, there are considerable complementarities that can be developed in bilateral trade and investment flows.

Other Asian emerging markets also offer considerable potential for Japan, including Indonesia, where Japanese automakers are investing heavily in building up auto production capacity to meet fast-growing demand for autos and commercial vehicles.

Therefore given Japan's own domestic market is now entering a period of stagnation and decline due to ageing demographics and the declining population, the future of Japan lies in greater engagement with emerging Asia, across a wide range of both manufacturing and service sector exports. While large Japanese multinationals have been very globalised for decades, small to medium enterprises will generally need to become far more engaged in seeking new markets globally, often in emerging markets where conditions are unfamiliar and difficult. Young Japanese entering the workforce will probably need to be far more engaged with emerging markets than previous generations, whether that means doing business in emerging Africa or Latin America or focusing on tourists visiting Japan from developing Asia or the Middle East.

If Japan can adapt to the changing Asia-Pacific landscape and develop new international competitiveness in segments of the service sector such as financial services and tourism, then the economic prospects for Japan to emerge from its current malaise would improve considerably.

One important cultural change that is evident to me in Japan today is a very different attitude towards the rest of Asia compared to twenty years ago. I feel a completely different attitude towards other Asians both from senior executives and young Japanese. Japanese today seem to be much more closely engaged with the rest of Asia, and I no longer feel there is any sense of condescending attitudes towards other Asians. The younger generations of Japanese have a much stronger interest and empathy with emerging Asian countries. This is a very crucial cultural change, putting Japan in a much stronger competitive position for the Asian Century and for being a leading partner in future Asian political and economic co-operation initiatives .

To avoid becoming the next Greece, Japan must not only rely on fiscal consolidation, but also on strategies to improve the long-term potential economic growth rate back above 2 per cent real GDP growth per year. If the Japanese corporate sector, especially at small to medium enterprise level, can become more outward-looking and actively build up their trade and investment in emerging Asia, the 'Land of the Rising Sun' need not become the 'Land of the Setting Sun'.

Chapter 8

Indonesia

Asia's next BRIC economy

Indonesia is one of the unheralded and unremarked success stories in the region politically in the last 20 years. The transformation from a military dictatorship as late as in 1998 to what is the third largest democracy in the world is remarkable.

John Howard, Former Prime Minister of Australia,
on-the-record interview with author at RSIS Singapore
Global Dialogue, 2010.

The new republic under Sukarno and Suharto

'Sukarno feed your people.' In one of the most haunting moments of Peter Weir's acclaimed 1982 film 'The Year of Living Dangerously', the photographer Billy Kwan hangs out a banner with these words in his desperation at his country's plight, as President Sukarno's motorcade approaches. His protest is in vain, as Indonesian security police break into his hotel room and throw him out of the window to his death before the motorcade arrives. The film – based on a book by the same name written by Christopher Koch – was banned from being shown in Indonesia until 1999.

Indonesia in 1965, as depicted in Peter Weir's film, was a nation in which the majority of the population lived in abject poverty, with teeming slums throughout the capital city of Jakarta. Estimated average GDP per person was only USD 55 per year. Even by 1970, average GDP had only risen to USD 82 per year, according to United Nations Statistical Division calculations based on national accounts estimates.

To a large extent, Indonesia's poverty in 1965 could still be attributed to its long history of Dutch colonial rule. The Dutch had deliberately avoided creating the institutional structures for self-government or sufficient higher educational systems for their Indonesian subjects, quite unlike the model that British colonial governance had established elsewhere in Asia, such as Malaya, Hong Kong or India. The Indonesian economy had been moulded into an economic structure based on exports of plantation crops and mineral commodities, in order to serve the commercial requirements of its Dutch colonial masters, with around three-quarters of the workforce employed in the agricultural sector. Manufacturing and services remained relatively weak sectors of the economy.

However, a large share of responsibility for Indonesia's weak pace of economic development after independence was also attributable to President Sukarno, Indonesia's first president. Although Sukarno was one of the new nation's national heroes for his role in the struggle for independence from Dutch colonial rule, his achievements as a leader of the independence movement were subsequently tarnished by his poor record in economic development. From the time of independence until President Sukarno was ousted in 1966, the nation followed a growth model heavily influenced by socialist economic policies and a focus on protectionism. Per capita income in Indonesia between 1957 and 1965 showed no increase in nominal terms, a tremendous failure in human development terms. This was the grinding poverty portrayed in 'The Year of Living Dangerously'.

This failure of economic policy post-independence was hardly unique to Indonesia. Other large developing countries such as India and Egypt had also pursued socialist economic development policies, with similarly poor results. Nevertheless, the implications for the vast majority of Indonesia's population were that they remained mired in poverty and their nation remained one of the poorest in the world.

It was only when General Suharto assumed power after crushing the attempted PKI coup attempt in 1965 that the Indonesian economy began to show more dynamic economic growth. Suharto, who had ruthlessly purged Indonesia of communist sympathisers after the failed 30th September Movement coup, had naturally sought to forge a closer alliance with the West to support the Indonesian military in their anti-communist efforts. This was a crucial strategic alliance that the US and the UK welcomed, as a lynchpin in their own efforts to combat the rise of communism in Southeast Asia. For the UK, there was an additional important strategic advantage in this new alliance with Indonesia, as it rapidly defused the military confrontation between Indonesia and Britain over Malaysia. President Suharto became a central ally in the West's efforts to hold back the communist tide in Asia, and this relationship flowed through into strong Western support for Indonesia's economic development.

This close strategic relationship with the West, particularly with the US, was instrumental in the transformation of Indonesia's economic policy. Having inherited an economy that was essentially bankrupt and heavily indebted in terms of foreign debt, Suharto created a new partnership with the West, getting new flows of foreign aid from key bilateral economic partners, notably the US and Japan, but also from multilateral sources such as the World Bank. There was also strong engagement with the West in terms of economic policy-making, with Indonesia embarking on a programme of economic liberalisation that helped to catalyse an improved economic performance.

Importantly, a generation of Indonesian technocrats studied economics in US universities – what became known as Indonesia's 'Berkeley mafia' – creating the underpinnings for a shift towards more market-oriented economic policy-making.

Suharto was also helped by several serendipitous events in the world economy that were to strongly benefit Indonesia for many years. Firstly, the world oil price shocks of 1973 and 1979 forced world prices sharply higher, which was very beneficial to Indonesia as it was a significant oil and gas exporting nation at that time. The sharp rise in world oil prices boosted Indonesia's oil and gas revenues significantly, giving the Indonesian government considerably more scope to undertake ambitious social and economic development programmes.

Equally important was the Green Revolution in global agriculture, as international agricultural researchers developed new rice strains that significantly improved the productivity of rice farmers. With rice being the key staple food crop for Indonesia, this helped to ensure food security for a generation. Indonesian rice production grew at an average annual rate of 4.5 per cent per year between 1965 and 1989.

Industrial development also progressed significantly, with manufacturing virtually doubling its contribution to GDP from 12.7 per cent in 1983 to 22.3 per cent by 1993. To support the growth of the agricultural sector, fertiliser production increased from 100,000 tonnes in 1969 to 6 million tonnes by 1993.

The decline of Suharto's new order
and the East Asian crisis

Despite the significant economic progress made during the initial years of Suharto's presidency, the Indonesian economy fell into a period of prolonged political and economic crisis for almost a decade from 1997 until 2004, reflecting domestic economic imbalances and political fault lines that had built up over many years but were rapidly exposed during the East Asian economic crisis.

One factor that contributed to the deteriorating economic situation was the decline in global oil prices during the 1980s, which reduced the flow of fiscal revenues that had helped fund Indonesia's economic development. The rise of crony capitalism under Suharto's rule also became an increasingly negative factor for the Indonesian business sector, as Suharto's family and his close business associates obtained stakes in many of Indonesia's key industries, amassing large fortunes.

Although the Indonesian economy appeared to still be showing relatively sustained strong growth during the early 1990s, the vulnerabilities were increasing.

In August 1997, the Indonesian economy became engulfed in the East Asian crisis, as contagion spread from Thailand to other East Asian economies with significant economic imbalances. Indonesia's vulnerabilities included very high levels of external debt and relatively limited foreign exchange reserves. As investors became increasingly concerned about the spreading contagion of the East Asian crisis, East Asian currencies, including the Indonesian rupiah, were sold off as investors sought the safe havens of the US dollar, Japanese yen and other major reserve currencies. The rupiah began to depreciate sharply, creating mounting problems for the large Indonesian corporations which had leveraged their balance sheets with substantial foreign currency borrowings. As the flight of global capital from East Asia intensified and the economic crisis worsened, the Indonesian economy began to fall into a vicious downward spiral of currency depreciation and rising inflation. The rupiah depreciated from around 2,500 per US dollar in July 1997 to around 14,000 per US dollar by January 1998.

As the Indonesian economy fell into a deep recession and large corporations were unable to service their debts, a banking sector crisis unfolded which resulted in the closure of sixteen commercial banks by November 1997, and a run on banking system deposits during December 1997 that affected many Indonesian banks, with the Indonesian financial system having become insolvent and coming close to total collapse. This was staved off by an emergency financial sector programme announced by the government in January 1998, which guaranteed bank deposits, together with another programme under which the government would undertake banking sector restructuring. The IMF provided a series of bail-outs to Indonesia, with a total of USD 43 billion in IMF loans provided by 1998. Many banks were taken over by the government or recapitalised, and the banking sector went through a protracted period of consolidation and restructuring.

Suharto's crony capitalist regime, which had been increasingly the focus of public ire even during the earlier years of relatively strong growth, now came into the spotlight as the Indonesian economy fell into this deep crisis. By March 1998, after his re-election by an unrepresentative parliament to another five-year term and his appointment of family members and key business associates to cabinet posts, the streets of Jakarta became the stage for violent anti-Suharto protests.

Despite Suharto's attempt to appease the nation by announcing a reorganisation of his government at the beginning of May 1998, the situation descended into ugly violence, as Indonesian youths turned their wrath against the ethnic Chinese population. The Chinese community played an important role in Indonesian commerce, which had given rise to long-standing resentment by some segments of Indonesia's ethnic majority population, particularly due to some close business ties between prominent ethnic Chinese entrepreneurs and the Suharto business empire.

The anti-Chinese riots spread through a number of cities and towns in Indonesia, including Jakarta, with the death toll estimated to have exceeded 1,000 persons, with widespread looting of Chinese properties. With the turbulent political situation and worsening economic crisis, there was significant capital flight out of Indonesia, and many wealthy individuals sought safe havens abroad for their financial assets.

Faced with the increasingly chaotic situation and his own rising unpopularity, Suharto resigned on 21st May 1998. He and his family remained in Jakarta until his death in January 2008. Although there were various government efforts to prosecute him for corruption, he was never convicted, although his son Tommy Suharto was convicted of corruption charges in an Indonesian court and served a prison term.

Indonesia entered a period of protracted political instability and weak economic performance for the next six years, with successive Indonesian leaders struggling to stabilise the situation. It was not until Yudhoyono was elected president in 2004 that Indonesia began to mount a sustained economic recovery.

The next Asian BRIC?

Since the East Asian crisis in 1997–98, which plunged the Indonesian economy into a deep recession and a period of considerable economic instability, Indonesia has emerged like a phoenix from the ashes. Indeed, Indonesia is now considered by many economists and international financial markets investors to be the next BRIC economy, fit to join the elite grouping of large, rapidly growing emerging market economies of Brazil, Russia, India and China.

Indonesia's position as one of the world's largest emerging markets has also increased its role as a key player in global geopolitics, winning it a seat at the G-20, the new forum for international decision-making, as well as at the BIS Basel Committee since 2009, giving it a greater voice in global decision-making on international financial standards-setting.

When President Susilo Bambang Yudhoyono (SBY) was elected to lead the Indonesian government in 2004, Indonesian GDP per person was just USD 1,200, which was virtually unchanged compared with 1995. The decade 1995–2004 was a period that had delivered little, if any, progress for the Indonesian people from a human development perspective, while there had also been considerable political instability. Indonesia had become mired in a period of economic stagnation. GDP per person had fallen sharply during the East Asian crisis in 1997–98, with Indonesia in political and economic turmoil. Indeed, when SBY took office, the economic future of Indonesia looked precarious, with risks that continued weak economic growth could result in protracted political and economic instability and further social unrest.

However, within the seven-year period since President SBY took office in 2004, GDP per capita in Indonesia had more than doubled, to around USD 3,000, reflecting the remarkable economic transformation that has taken place in Indonesia under his leadership. The medium-term outlook is for further progress in boosting per capita incomes, with GDP per person projected to exceed USD 5,000 by the end of 2015 based on current economic growth rates in the 6–7 per cent range.

As a result, global financial investors are increasingly discussing the possibility that Indonesia should be included among the BRIC economies, the largest, fast-growing emerging economies in the world. This has also been reflected in capital flows, with both foreign direct investment (FDI) and portfolio capital flows strengthening significantly in 2010 and 2011 due to growing international investor confidence in the Indonesian economic outlook.

Nevertheless, Indonesia remains a country facing tremendous further challenges in achieving fundamental human development goals. Despite progress in poverty reduction since 2004, the World Bank estimates that 32 million Indonesians live in poverty, with half of all households close to the national poverty line. Rural poverty remains a burgeoning problem, with the rural poor accounting for around 70 per cent of the total numbers in poverty. Similarly, despite large improvements in the access to basic health care since 2004, with health insurance coverage for the poor having roughly tripled to cover around 43 per cent of the population, this still leaves half of the poorest segments of society without access to basic health care cover.

However, President SBY's government made important economic progress during his first term in office, setting the foundations for sustainable development and poverty reduction. Substantial progress with macroeconomic reforms took place during the first term of his presidency, with the support of his able economic frontbench led by Sri Mulyani Indrawati.

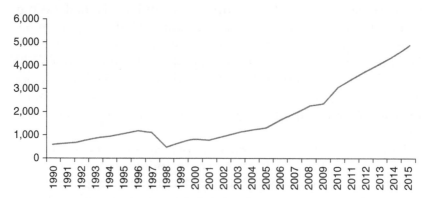

Figure 8.1 Indonesia: GDP per capita, US dollars
Sources: Indonesian Government Statistics, IMF forecasts.

The macroeconomic achievements of his economic frontbench during his first term of office have included substantial achievements in reducing the twin burdens of high government debt and external debt over the last seven years. Government debt as a share of GDP has been reduced from 56 per cent of GDP in 2004 to an estimated 25 per cent of GDP by 2011, putting Indonesia's government debt burden in a very favourable light compared with the fiscal plight of most OECD countries today.

Against the global background of sharply higher government debt to GDP ratios in many OECD countries since the 2008–09 global financial crisis, Indonesia's government debt burden is very low compared with most other developed and developing nations, and indeed continued to decline even through the 2008–09 crisis, despite the global recession. A crucial underpinning for this strong fiscal performance has been the substantial reforms undertaken to strengthen the banking system since the East Asian crisis. As noted in the IMF's Article IV consultation in 2011, Indonesia has made great progress over the last decade in improving financial sector stability and strengthening bank regulation and supervision.

The Indonesian economic frontbench also demonstrated their skilful economic management through the global financial crisis in 2008–09, when international financial markets expected Indonesia to experience an external account crisis, as it had during the East Asian crisis. Indeed, in late 2008, Indonesian CDS spreads – a measure of risk of sovereign default – had risen to more than 1,200 basis points, signalling that global financial markets feared an Indonesian crisis was imminent.

However, the government acted pre-emptively by arranging a USD 5.5 billion contingent financing facility with the World Bank and other international development agencies, while a further USD 3 billion was raised through a sovereign bond issue, strengthening Indonesia's external account position considerably, and helping it to sail through the global economic tempests.

Indonesia's economic resilience was further demonstrated by the positive 4.6 per cent GDP growth rate recorded in 2009, a year when many countries worldwide, including some in East Asia, suffered deep recessions.

Indonesia's external account position has also improved substantially, with external debt as a share of GDP having been reduced from 54 per cent of GDP in 2004 to around 23 per cent of GDP in 2010, another very significant achievement in reducing Indonesia's vulnerability to external financing. This improved

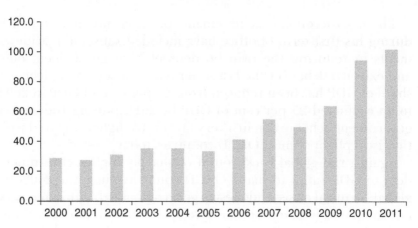

Figure 8.2   Indonesian foreign exchange reserves, USD billion
Source: Bank Indonesia.

external account position has also been strengthened by a significant rise in foreign exchange reserves since 2004. In 2004,
Indonesia's FX reserves were around USD 35 billion, and since
then have tripled, breaking through the USD 100 billion mark in
early 2011 and hitting US 110 billion by February 2012, equivalent
to around 6 months' import cover.

The roadmap for reform

Despite the many positive macroeconomic developments that have
occurred in Indonesia over the last seven years, the economic
development path ahead remains very long and challenging. The
nation continues to face many significant problems, such as the
high level of corruption, an uncertain legal environment, difficult
labour laws and a complex environment for FDI. Despite rapidly
rising GDP levels per capita, Indonesia continues to face high
levels of poverty amongst its population. Poverty is particularly
concentrated amongst the rural population, and regional inequalities of income have left some regions of Indonesia very far behind
national average income levels.

A key vulnerability facing Indonesia is the youthful demographic profile and its implications for the workforce over coming decades. Over the next ten years, Indonesia's working age
population is set to rise by around 20 million persons. This
means that Indonesia will need to generate around 2 million
net new jobs each year for its growing workforce, or face the

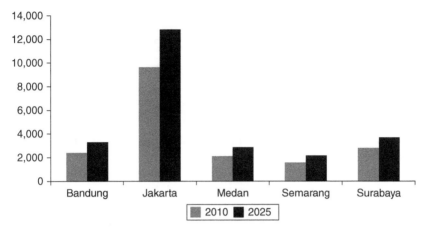

Figure 8.3 Largest Indonesian cities: population, in 2010 and 2025, in thousands
Source: UN, World Urbanisation Prospects, 2011.

risk of rising discontent and social unrest. As the Arab Spring in the Middle East and North Africa has shown, such tensions can remain dormant for an extended period of time, but can suddenly flare up into political unrest in a very short time frame if the underlying social conditions – such as high unemployment and poverty levels – breed discontent.

An important focus for Indonesia over the medium- to long-term is therefore to create a dynamic, entrepreneurial economy that is capable of generating a wide range of jobs in many sectors of the economy, ranging from skilled professionals to vocationally qualified blue collar workers as well as unskilled labour.

Due to its rapid population growth, Indonesia will face challenges related to the future growth of its cities, particularly Jakarta, which will be Indonesia's only megacity by 2025. Nevertheless other large Indonesian cities will also be experiencing rapid population growth. As with China and India, a key priority will therefore be to build modern urban infrastructure and create smart cities for future urban development that also integrate modern smart grid technology.

Jakarta faces very significant environmental risks due to its vulnerability to flooding as well as the impact of climate change, as sea levels rise. At present, flooding due to heavy rainfall has been a persistent problem for many years. Major flooding of Jakarta occurred in February 2007 after heavy rainfall brought large volumes of water through the river systems that run through Jakarta and its hinterland. Heavy infrastructure investment will therefore be needed over the next decade to mitigate the risks to Jakarta from flooding.

While the Indonesian mineral resources sector, notably minerals and energy, has a vital role to play in Indonesia's future economic development, in general it is relatively capital intensive and is unlikely to generate sufficient direct and indirect employment growth in the economy to match the pace of growth of the workforce. Therefore, a crucial element of Indonesia's future economic development to create a well-diversified economy is to build a strong, competitive manufacturing sector that can generate substantial growth in employment. A key focus must also be on regional economic development, so that the benefits of growth accrue across the regions of Indonesia, to address issues of regional income inequalities and rural poverty.

Creating the enabling business environment to encourage the growth of manufacturing, through investment by both domestic and foreign entrepreneurs, is a key role for government. Indonesia has in many ways been a laggard compared to many East Asian countries in terms of creating a competitive business culture that encourages both large multinationals as well as small to medium enterprises to establish operations and compete in domestic and international markets.

With Indonesia's urban population set to continue to rise rapidly over the next two decades, the need for sustained job creation in the manufacturing and service sectors will be important for social stability and to avoid inner city problems related to high unemployment and urban decay.

Therefore a key priority for the Indonesian government must be to accelerate the pace of economic reforms for business, to create a more competitive environment that allows privately owned small and medium businesses to become an important force for job creation. At the same time, barriers to international investment and foreign competition need to continue to be lowered. This will not only help to generate more private sector jobs in both manufacturing and service sectors, but will also gradually lift productivity and the long-term potential growth rate of the economy.

At present, the Indonesian economy has shown sustained ability to deliver growth of around 6 per cent per year, but has struggled to lift average annual growth much above that. In order for Indonesia to accelerate the pace of economic development and improve human development conditions more rapidly, lifting the potential growth rate to around 8 per cent GDP per year is a key priority.

A number of key strategic initiatives are essential to allow this to happen.

Firstly, a major government initiative to accelerate the pace of microeconomic reforms is required in order to deliver sustained improvements to economic competition in the Indonesian economy. This includes major reforms of state-owned enterprises, to ensure they are operating in a more transparent manner and that key sectors they operate in are liberalised and opened up to market competition.

Secondly, the pace of infrastructure investment needs to increase substantially. The Indonesian government has already identified this as a key policy objective, having set a target of catalysing around USD 120 billion of infrastructure investment over the current five-year national development plan, requiring around USD 24 billion of infrastructure investment per year. The Indonesian government has estimated that it has the capacity to fund around 30 per cent of this, with much of the remainder coming from private investment and public-private partnership projects. In 2011, the Indonesian government included a very substantial increase in infrastructure spending in its fiscal budget, amounting to an increase of around 48 per cent. This reflected a new sense of urgency about the need for infrastructure development as a catalyst for economic development. Despite these government initiatives, the private sector will need to play a central role in financing Indonesian infrastructure development over the long term. A significant portion of the private sector financing will need to be externally funded, and therefore creating an attractive long-term environment for FDI is essential. While the process of legal reforms is underway, substantial further liberalisation of the FDI environment is also important.

Thirdly, major new initiatives are required to develop human capital. A major competitive weakness of Indonesia that was a legacy of Dutch colonial rule but has since persisted despite over half a century of independence is the weakness of the educational system. Successive Indonesian post-independence governments have lacked focus in building a strong educational system, both in terms of vocational education and higher, tertiary-level educational institutions. This persistent policy failing has severely hampered Indonesia's economic development and its economic competitiveness, creating significant bottlenecks for industrial development. Greater involvement of foreign educational institutions as partners to Indonesian educational institutions in secondary and tertiary

education as well as vocational training could accelerate the process of improving educational standards in Indonesia.

For the manufacturing and services sectors to flourish, creating
a modern and skilled workforce is critical. This requires substantial efforts to build up tertiary and vocational training institutions
in the major urban centres of Indonesia, assisted and catalysed
by joint ventures and partnerships with foreign universities and
technical training institutes. This will be a critical component of
increasing the international competitiveness of Indonesia as an
attractive destination for FDI, as well as enabling domestic firms
to compete more effectively in international markets. Under
President SBY, the process of strengthening Indonesia's educational systems has accelerated, but it will take many years for
the results of these improvements to have a significant impact on
Indonesia's economy.

Risks and vulnerabilities

Indonesia is on the threshold of becoming one of the world's
major emerging market economies. However, it also faces significant risks and vulnerabilities, due to the need to ensure that the
benefits of economic development flow through into rising living
standards for all sections of society.

Political risk remains an important concern. With Indonesian
President SBY having played a crucial role in encouraging the
fledgling democratic process in Indonesia as well as delivering
very significant macroeconomic achievements, a key risk is that
the economic reform process will lose momentum after he steps
down when his second and final term of office ends, which is
scheduled to be in 2014.

If the new president and cabinet of Indonesia do not maintain
the same commitment to macroeconomic soundness and broader
economic reforms, then Indonesia could again face economic difficulties and a weaker pace of economic growth, as well as the
disillusionment of foreign investors.

Given the still large share of the Indonesian population that
live in poverty, there are significant downside political risks over
the medium to long term if the pace of economic development
cannot be sustained. A key risk is Indonesia's young demographic
profile, with a large number of youth due to enter the labour force
over the next twenty years. If the economic growth momentum is

insufficient to generate enough jobs for the youth cohorts entering the workforce, then there is a significant risk of social unrest,
as seen in North Africa in 2011.

There is also the risk that if the growth path of the Indonesian
economy should lose momentum for any significant period of
time, the mounting social unrest could support a resurgence of
Islamic fundamentalist groups, including an increased threat
from terrorist organisations.

To illustrate the point about the simmering political tensions
that exist in many developing countries, including Indonesia, I
can relate a personal experience of how unrest can flare up. With
marvellous bad timing, I flew from Singapore into Jakarta on
the morning that the Bali bombers were executed in November
2008. I still recall seeing a televised statement by the Australian
foreign minister at the time, Stephen Smith, which was being
shown repeatedly on Singapore TV channels that morning as I
was about to head to the airport. In his statement, he was broadcasting a warning to Australian citizens not to travel to Indonesia
if possible, due to risk of reprisals. This was hardly a reassuring
start to my journey to Jakarta.

I was picked up at Jakarta's Soekarno-Hatta Airport by a hotel
car from a large international hotel group which wisely was completely unmarked. The wisdom of that precaution became evident
soon after, when the car, en route to the city, entered a roundabout
where a swarm of angry youth protestors wearing headbands
mobbed the car, bringing it to a complete halt. They surrounded
the car and peered inside the windows. Seeing only an Indonesian
driver and another Asian with dark skin like their own sitting in
the back, they waved us on. I often wonder what would have happened if a Westerner had been in the car.

The sequel to this story is that the country head of the firm
I was working for at the time met with me the next morning
and also warned me to avoid likely targets for reprisals. When I
asked which places were 'likely targets', I was told to avoid large
US hotel chains, bars where a lot of Australians hang out, as
well as the international airport. I seemed to have ticked two of
these three boxes already since I was staying in a well-known US
hotel chain and obviously had to use the international airport.
I made it a full house later that evening when, while trying to
exercise caution, I decided to remain in the hotel and went to the
lounge for a drink. I found myself surrounded by a large group
of Australians. So I managed to tick all three boxes of the things

I had been told a foreigner should not do in Jakarta! I was relieved at the time to find that all the Australians in the hotel lounge seemed to be Australian Federal Police officers, so I felt very safe, but looking back I am not sure if that perhaps made us an even more obvious target for some plotters.

During that visit to Jakarta in late 2008, I attended a business conference organised by The Economist Group, which publishes *The Economist* magazine, a much respected organisation that I would later work for. At that conference I met many local business leaders and foreign business executives working for multinationals in Jakarta. Nine months later, some of the same people I had met were killed or wounded in a bomb blast at the JW Marriott Hotel in Jakarta. A suicide bomber had managed to enter the hotel despite tight security and detonated himself at a business forum for Jakarta-based executives of multinationals organised by CastleAsia, run by an eminent foreign analyst of Indonesia, James Castle. Castle himself was injured, but I met him about a year later and fortunately he seemed to have recovered very well.

I mention these incidents to highlight that political risk is still a key consideration in Indonesia, and that despite the significant economic progress there is no room for complacency about the potential for social unrest and turbulence that could surface if the economy does not continue to sustain strong growth.

With a large share of Indonesian households still living close to the poverty line, there is a pressing urgency to catalysing physical infrastructure spending as well as human capital development to lift Indonesia's potential growth rate from around 6 per cent currently to around 8 per cent or higher over the medium term, so as to accelerate the pace of economic development and poverty reduction.

A trillion dollar consumer market

Indonesia won its spurs amongst the global financial community during the global financial crisis in 2008–09. It weathered the global economic storm with positive GDP growth of 4.6 per cent in 2009, followed by GDP growth of 6.1 per cent in 2010. By 2011, the economy grew at its fastest since the East Asian crisis, with the pace of growth reaching 6.5 per cent. The resilient economic performance during the global financial crisis and strong growth since 2009 has significantly enhanced Indonesia's credentials with global investors, particularly as the strong macroeconomic track record has remained in place, with low fiscal deficits and government debt levels sustained since 2008.

As a result, both Moody's and Fitch had upgraded Indonesia to investment grade ratings for its sovereign external debt in 2011, even as many European countries received significant downgrades in credit ratings. Indeed, in late 2011, interest rate spreads for Indonesian sovereign bond issuances in global markets had declined to below spreads for some major European countries that were in the centre of the EU sovereign debt crisis, such as Italy and Spain.

The economic outlook for Indonesia is for potential growth of around 6–7 per cent per year over the medium term. This is projected to drive Indonesian GDP through the USD 1 trillion mark by 2015, reinforcing Indonesia's position as one of the largest developing economies in the world. Importantly, the size of its domestic consumer market is also expected to surpass the trillion dollar mark within the next decade, making it an increasingly attractive economy for large multinationals, as sustained strong economic growth and its youthful demographic profile drive consumer expenditure.

A key driver of Indonesia's growth over the long term will be the strong demand from China and India for both agricultural and mineral resources from Indonesia, boosted by rapid growth in consumer expenditure in both those countries. This is already attracting significant direct investment flows into Indonesia from Chinese and Indian resources firms that are keen to secure supply lines for key commodities.

The growing economic weight of the Indonesian economy amongst the group of developing nations has also lifted the geopolitical importance of Indonesia. This is reflected in its new seat since 2009 as a member of the G-20, which has become the main global international forum for economic decision-making for the world economy, as well as its new seat on the BIS Basel Committee, the key international standards-setting body for the global financial services industry. This has considerably increased its international political weight, a trend which is expected to continue over coming decades.

This has most significance within the ASEAN region. Indonesia's position as the largest economy amongst the ASEAN countries, together with the impact of its sustained economic expansion on trade and investment flows with other ASEAN members, has made Indonesia an increasingly important driving force for the future economic growth of the ASEAN region. As the size of the Indonesian domestic market continues to expand rapidly, with total GDP projected to exceed USD 2 trillion by 2022, Indonesia is expected to propel ASEAN to become one of the fastest-growing regions of the global economy over the medium to long term.

The Indonesian economy is rapidly becoming an important market opportunity for ASEAN companies, creating a wide range of business opportunities for ASEAN trade partners. For example, Malaysian financial services firms, including the large banking giants CIMB and Maybank, are expanding into the Indonesian financial services market, notably the fast-growing Islamic financial services sector. A wide range of other Malaysian firms invest in Indonesia in resources sectors such as palm oil and coal. Singaporean firms are involved in a wide range of investments in construction, infrastructure and urban development projects as well as in natural resources projects in Indonesia. Such investments by ASEAN multinationals seeking to tap the business opportunities in Indonesia are set to grow rapidly over the next decade.

If the strong economic performance of Indonesia since 2004 can be sustained, with average annual GDP growth over the next decade of over 6 per cent per year, Indonesia will continue to be one of Asia's fastest-growing consumer markets. This will also make Indonesia an increasingly important contributor to Asia-Pacific economic growth, trade and investment flows. Indeed, Indonesia is well positioned to become the next BRIC country, creating a third Asian growth engine after China and India for the Asia-Pacific region and an important driver for the rapid economic development of ASEAN.

As the size of the Indonesian economy continues to grow and it joins the ranks of the world's largest economies, this will also result in Indonesia becoming an increasingly important player in global geopolitics, as well as an important central lynchpin for the political and economic cooperation of ASEAN as a bloc of nations.

Indonesia is a great nation with rich cultural wealth and Indonesians are amongst the most polite and friendly people anywhere in the world. If Indonesia takes its rightful place as a global leader on the world stage, it should be a very positive development for ASEAN as a whole as well as for emerging markets globally, since Indonesia well understands the challenges of human development for low income countries.

In 1955, Sukarno had become the leader of a grouping of developing countries that had made a commitment to achieving world peace and cooperation in the Bandung Conference of Asian and African countries, which came to be known as the Bandung Declaration. That brought few, if any, tangible results but seemed merely to be a political form of 'wayang kulit' – Indonesia's traditional shadow puppet theatre.

However, the time may finally have come for Indonesia to truly take up a global leadership role to champion the cause of developing countries worldwide, backed up by its rapidly increasing economic strength as it becomes one of the world's leading emerging markets and joins the ranks of the BRIC nations.

Chapter 9

Wild, wild East

Asia's new frontier economies

> We just want to improve the state of Burma. ... It is national commitment that will bring us both national reconciliation and improvements in our material condition.
>
> Daw Aung San Suu Kyi, Speech at World Economic Forum,
> Bangkok, June 2012.

The Burma Road: Asia's next tiger economy

In the last twenty years, I have given thousands of presentations and briefings about the Asia-Pacific economies to senior executives of global multinationals as well as to government and business delegations from many countries worldwide. In these meetings I have been asked questions about most of the Asia-Pacific countries at some point, but in all this time, nobody had ever asked me about the Myanmar economy. It was so isolated from the global economy by the autarkic policies of its own repressive government as well as by international sanctions that it hardly existed in the minds of investors.

However, that suddenly changed. It changed for me on a memorable occasion, at an international conference on regional security and defence policy, the IISS Shangri-La Dialogue in Singapore in 2010. I found myself seated at dinner next to the Myanmar ambassador to Singapore. Having previously lived in Burma for five years, and with my sister having been born in Rangoon, the progress of Myanmar is of special interest to me. For the first time in decades, I found I was having a conversation about the Myanmar economy, albeit rather briefly, as our discussions gave way for South Korean President Lee Myung-bak, as he took the podium to give his keynote speech. Tensions on the Korean peninsula were high and the issue dominated the 2010 IISS Shangri-La Dialogue, which is focused on Asia-Pacific regional security issues. Discussion on our table about Myanmar soon switched to the Korean military and political risks.

I could not in my wildest dreams have imagined that exactly two years later, on the very eve of the 2012 IISS Shangri-La Dialogue, I would meet 'The Lady', the Burmese Nobel Peace Prize Laureate and leader of the Burmese people's non-violent struggle for democracy, Aung San Suu Kyi. When I was invited to speak at the World Economic Forum in Bangkok in 2012, I was thrilled to find that 'The Lady' would be a keynote speaker, and I hoped to be able to at least see her for the first time when she was speaking.

Events turned out in a more unlikely way, when I found that instead of me attending her speech, she was attending mine. I saw her sitting in the front row of the audience for my WEF panel session and took the opportunity to meet her. Truly a serendipitous event for me. Of course, I did attend her very moving keynote speech later, which was her first major international speech since leaving Burma for the first time in over two decades and was widely reported by the international media.

Since 2011 investor interest in Myanmar has escalated. I now find that there is hardly any meeting with multinationals or investors where Myanmar does not come up on the list of hot topics for discussion. I have found over the years that a great indicator for what's hot and what is not is hotel occupancy. Back in 2003–04 when the India boom was really getting underway, my relatives and friends in New Delhi started commenting about how full the famous Delhi hotels were, with large numbers of foreign business visitors evident in their lobbies and restaurants. By 2007, booking a hotel room at a good Mumbai or Delhi hotel became a challenge, even at exorbitant prices.

Yangon is not exactly Delhi or Mumbai, but since 2011, its hotels are also filled with foreign business visitors and foreign delegations. Yangon's grand old hotels, such as the Strand, are now charging premium rates for ordinary hotel rooms due to the shortage of good quality hotel accommodation and the flood of foreign business visitors. In many Asian countries I visit, business executives speak of their own recent company visits or official national business delegation visits to Myanmar.

Although Myanmar had been out of focus for decades, its strategic importance has been evident since the Pacific War. During the Second World War, Burma became an important battleground for the Allies in their attempt to halt the sweeping Japanese victories across the Asia-Pacific. Burma was crucial for a number of reasons. Firstly, it was the last buffer between the Japanese and Britain's prized colony of India. Secondly, Burma provided the last open supply route from the sea to provide essential military equipment to the Chinese military to stem the Japanese advance in China. Today, as China's economy has become increasingly dependent on imported raw materials and commodities, particularly energy imports, the strategic importance of Myanmar to China is again becoming evident. For India, Myanmar is also of great strategic importance, as a key buffer state between southern China and the India border.

From the Chinese perspective, the strategic importance of Myanmar was also proven during the Pacific War. After the Japanese invasion of China in 1937, the Burma Road from the Burmese capital of Rangoon to Kunming in southern China became the critically important supply route for China, after Japanese forces captured all of the Chinese coastal provinces. The US government used the Burma Road to provide essential military supplies to the Chinese government, to support their efforts to block the Japanese advance. When the Burma Road was eventually cut off by the Japanese invasion of Burma in 1942, the Allied military supplies to China could no longer get through.

This resulted in the construction of the Ledo Road from Ledo in the Indian state of Assam to a section of the Burma Road that was still under Allied control, opening the land supply route again to Kunming in China. While the Ledo Road was being built by US Army engineers, the famous air corridor over 'the hump' was used by the US 14th Air Force under the command of General Claire Chennault to airlift supplies to the Chinese military forces. The Ledo Road was built by the US Army troops in Assam under the command of General 'Vinegar Joe' Stilwell, and was eventually renamed the Stilwell Road.

Today, the supply route from the Burmese coast up to southern China has again taken on heightened significance as security of resources supply becomes increasingly important as a key strategic policy priority for China. The supply route through what is today known as Myanmar into southern China has become increasingly important for China both from the security and economic perspectives.

Firstly, using the Myanmar coastal ports as transshipment points into southern China significantly reduces the length of the transportation routes to supply inland provinces of southern China compared with freight shipments that go all the way through the Straits of Malacca and up into the South China Sea. This can potentially reduce shipment time as well as transport costs if the transport infrastructure is of sufficient standards.

Secondly, from a strategic perspective, the Straits of Malacca are a choke point for China's crucial oil supplies, and Burma offers an alternative transshipment point that is also logistically much shorter for the inland southern Chinese provinces than the shipping route from the Strait of Hormuz via the Straits of Malacca to the coastal Chinese ports.

The Myanmar to China supply chain helps China to mitigate the risks of the Straits of Malacca becoming a key choke point for Chinese shipping in the event of disruption to shipping lanes in the Straits of Malacca.

Thirdly, as the development of the inland provinces of China continues to move forward at a rapid pace, the Burma Road provides an important supply route for the rapidly growing trade flows between China and ASEAN, as well as a southern transport route for inland Chinese exports to the world.

As a result, increasingly Myanmar has become strategically important to China as a supply route. With energy security a key policy priority for China due to its rapidly growing energy imports of oil, natural gas and coal, Myanmar is important as a transshipment hub for oil and gas from the Myanmar coast into southern China, providing an alternative oil and gas supply route into China that avoids the need for ships to sail through the Straits of Malacca.

The role of Myanmar in China's energy security strategy has also heightened due to Myanmar's own oil and gas resources. Chinese firms have led international consortiums that have built oil and gas pipelines from the Shwe gas fields in offshore Myanmar into southern China. A USD 1.5 billion oil pipeline runs for 770 kilometres from Kyaukphyu in Myanmar to Kunming, with another USD 1 billion pipeline supplying natural gas from the Shwe fields to Kunming and further to Guizhou and Guanxi, running a total distance of 2,800 kilometres.

With considerable undeveloped oil and gas reserves, Myanmar's energy resources are of significance to China's energy security strategy. However, China's dominant role in Myanmar's economy over the last five decades has become an increasing source of discontent for the Myanmar government as well as the population, which have fears that China's influence has become too great. This has fanned nationalist sentiment, particularly about Chinese access to Myanmar's natural resources.

The decision in 2011 by the Myanmar government to halt the construction of one of the world's largest dam projects, which was being built and financed by Chinese companies to export hydro-electric power to China, became symbolic of the Myanmar government's own strategic shift in policy to diversify its international relationships.

Consequently, the Burmese government has sought to broaden its political and economic relationships beyond China. A key platform of its new international engagement is its membership of ASEAN. Other ASEAN members have been at the forefront of international efforts to strengthen regional political and economic relations with Myanmar. Following the election of Thein Sein as Myanmar's new president in 2011, ASEAN leaders made a key decision to allow Myanmar to become the ASEAN chair in 2014, an important political milestone for Myanmar.

However, Myanmar's membership of ASEAN also creates obligations. By 2015, Myanmar will need to significantly dismantle tariff barriers on goods in order to meet its commitments under the ASEAN Free Trade Agreement, a target that Vietnam, Laos and Cambodia will also have to meet at the same time in order to reach the same low tariff levels that have already been implemented by the original six members of ASEAN.

Furthermore, Myanmar will also need to make progress towards the goals for the creation of the ASEAN Economic Community by 2015, to the extent that other ASEAN members also move towards the implementation of these targets.

The new engagement between Myanmar and other ASEAN countries has already catalysed significant trade and investment interest in Myanmar by other companies in other ASEAN countries. There has been a stream of official business delegations led by ministers from other ASEAN countries that have visited Myanmar since early 2011, as well as significantly increased business activity by Asian firms seeking to position themselves for the rapid liberalisation of the Myanmar economy.

Consequently, there is growing international optimism that after decades of military government in Myanmar that had ruthlessly suppressed democracy and the development of a market economy, Myanmar is now moving on a path towards greater economic liberalisation and economic reforms, as well as some political reforms.

The decision by the Thein Sein government to permit opposition leader Aung San Suu Kyi and her National League for

Democracy (NLD) party to contest by-elections in April 2012 for a relatively small share of the total number of parliamentary seats resulted in sweeping electoral victories for her party in almost all of the contested seats, with the NLD winning 43 of the 45 seats contested.

Given the history of political repression by the military government for decades, including their refusal to implement the results of the 1990 election which the NLD won decisively, as well as the detention of Aung San Suu Kyi under house arrest for a total period of fifteen years, these latest political reforms have been welcomed by democracies worldwide as a sign of significant political change. This has been regarded by Western democracies as an important step forward in terms of political reforms, and consequently has triggered significant easing of Western political and economic sanctions on Myanmar.

The US government has restored full diplomatic relations with Myanmar, appointing Derek J. Mitchell as the US ambassador to Burma in 2012 (it remains US policy to refer to the country as 'Burma'), while both the US and EU have suspended most economic sanctions against Myanmar in the weeks following the April 2012 election. The US also eased sanctions on the export of financial services and new investments to Burma in July 2012.

However, a key risk is the major political hurdle that still lies ahead in 2015, when the Myanmar government has agreed to hold full parliamentary elections. If they realise they will be ousted from power by such an electoral process, it could trigger a split in the ruling regime or a political backlash prior to that date, which could result in political turmoil and a shift back to a more repressive regime.

However, while the political reform process continues and is regarded by the US, EU and other major democracies as credible, then it may pave the way for some gradual lifting of economic sanctions on Myanmar. This is likely to be a crucial catalyst for the accelerated economic development of Myanmar. The Myanmar government has put forward a very substantial agenda of key economic reforms, which already will be growth accelerants.

Myanmar has asked the IMF for assistance with policy advice for the reform of its dual exchange rate system, and has moved rapidly to implement a new, unified exchange rate system that entered into effect from April 2012. This exchange rate reform will be very important to improving Myanmar's trade and investment flows with the rest of the world, since prior to the unification of the exchange rate, the official rate had been 6 kyat per USD whereas the informal market rate was around 800 kyat, making it very unattractive for foreign firms to trade or invest at the official exchange rate.

A range of measures has been proposed in order to encourage foreign direct investment (FDI), including provision of five-year tax holidays and guarantees against nationalisation. With some of the economic sanctions by the US and EU having been suspended, and other Western democracies having lifted economic sanctions, the improved international political environment for FDI as well as the Myanmar government's own policy reforms could result in a significant upsurge in FDI flows.

The reasons for the heightened investor interest in Myanmar are manifold.

Firstly, Myanmar is a nation with significant oil and gas resources, and this is very attractive for energy companies looking for exploration and development opportunities. Myanmar already is producing oil and gas, and a number of new oil and gas exploration blocks have been awarded through international tender processes during 2011–12. While US and European sanctions have prevented Western oil companies from taking part in these tenders, Asian oil companies have been active in Myanmar, and many of the latest round of exploration blocks under tender have been awarded to Asian firms. Moreover, the world's fastest growing energy markets for decades to come – China and India – are on Myanmar's very doorstep, with Thailand also keen to secure Myanmar energy supplies for its own economy.

Secondly, Myanmar has a long history as one of the most productive rice-growing regions of Southeast Asia. Poor economic policies and attempts to create socialist systems to control the rice market resulted in a significant deterioration of Burma's rice production. However, this could rapidly recover with further market reforms and modern technology to improve rice quality and yields. If Myanmar can achieve significant gains in agricultural exports and these improved profits flow through to ordinary farmers, this could create significant gains in incomes for farmers, driving economic growth as well as reducing poverty levels.

Thirdly, Myanmar has been isolated from the global economy and has very poor physical infrastructure. If international development assistance flows help to trigger infrastructure development at a more rapid pace, this will also accelerate the pace of economic development. Momentum for re-establishment of development assistance flows is building rapidly, with the US having decided to establish a US Agency for International Development mission in Burma, while the World Bank and Asian Development Bank have re-opened their offices in Myanmar in August 2012. The World Bank has announced that it is considering providing USD 85 million in new development grants to Myanmar, while Japan is negotiating providing a loan to Myanmar to allow it to clear its debt arrears to the World Bank, which would allow new World Bank to begin subject to approval by World Bank shareholders. Japan itself has decided to forgo USD 3.7 billion of past loans owed and to resume full development assistance to Myanmar.

Fourthly, Myanmar has remained an economy that is heavily dependent on exports of agricultural and mineral resources, with little development of the manufacturing sector. Yet labour costs are low and the domestic market of an estimated 50 million people provides a large consumer market for manufacturers. Consequently, Myanmar could also become a more attractive location for investment in low-cost manufacturing, following a similar development path in the manufacturing sector to Cambodia and Vietnam.

Tourism to Myanmar is already increasing rapidly, and combined with the surge in business travel to Yangon, tourism will be a boom sector for Myanmar over the next decade if the government is willing to allow much increased tourism flows. This will create considerable opportunities for tourism-related investment in hotels, restaurants and other tourism facilities. Having often visited the Shwedagon Pagoda in Rangoon when I lived there, this alone is a splendid religious and touristic attraction that is sufficient reason for a tourist to visit Yangon.

Consequently, if the process of liberalisation is genuine, there could be a significant transformation of Myanmar's economic growth outlook. While the economy is currently showing the sustained ability to grow in the 5–6 per cent range, this growth rate could accelerate significantly over the medium term, similar to the experience of other Asian tiger economies over the last five decades.

However, the growth path of Myanmar will also face tremendous challenges, even with genuine political and economic reforms. If significant private foreign investment flows enter the Myanmar economy over the medium term, combined with increased inter-national development assistance, there is a clear risk that the econ-omy will not be able to absorb such rapid escalation in investment, triggering increased inflationary pressures.

Lacking a well-developed commercial banking and financial system, the ability of the central bank and government to tackle inflationary pressures will be heavily constrained, which could pose a significant risk to the ability of Myanmar to sustain its rapid growth path.

Therefore, it will be very important for the Myanmar gov-ernment to have full engagement by the IMF, World Bank and Asian Development Bank in developing its economic policy programme. Myanmar also has the significant advantage of its membership in ASEAN, and could and should therefore fully draw on the support of its ASEAN partners to provide assistance with economic development policy advice as well as advice on the appropriate measures to rapidly develop its financial system. Singapore and Malaysia are both highly successful financial cen-tres with amongst the best central banks worldwide, so Myanmar could draw on their help to move forward with its financial sec-tor development agenda. The +3 members of the ASEAN+3, Japan, South Korea and China, could also support Myanmar in these strategies.

Thus, Myanmar has plenty of Asian partner countries to turn to for policy assistance in framing its economic policy reforms, and these countries will mostly be quite eager to provide help to their ASEAN neighbour.

Corruption and poor governance are also key obstacles for the economic development outlook, and therefore the business climate will be difficult for foreign investors. However, this is clearly an issue in many developing countries around the world, and inter-national political pressure for reforms will need to be ongoing in this area to attempt to force changes.

A key weakness is the educational infrastructure and human capital of Myanmar. When Aung San Suu Kyi made her first major international speech outside of Myanmar after twenty-four years at the World Economic Forum in Bangkok in June 2012. I, like most of the audience in the room, was captivated by her integrity, sincerity and dedication of purpose. She highlighted the need for significant improvement in basic education standards in Burma, with a strong focus on secondary education, vocational train-ing and non-formal education, due to a lack of basic skills in the workforce to implement the economic reforms that the Myanmar government is implementing.

'The proportion of young people who are unemployed in Burma is extremely high. That, I keep saying, is a time bomb.'
    Daw Aung San Suu Kyi, Nobel Peace Prize Laureate and General Secretary of NLD Party of Myanmar, Speech at World Economic Forum, Bangkok, June 2012.

Despite the tremendous economic development challenges Myanmar will face, there is no doubt that the long-term outlook for Myanmar would be transformed by a shift to sustained political and economic liberalisation policies.

However, political risk in Myanmar remains very high, with considerable uncertainty about the willingness of the military government to pursue further significant political reforms. The outbreak of ethnic violence in Rakhine state between Buddhists and the ethnic minority Rohingya Muslims in 2012 further highlights the political risks in Myanmar.

With its vast natural resources, agricultural export potential and its large domestic consumer market for catalysing the growth of its manufacturing sector, Myanmar could become one of the most exciting economic development prospects for the 21st century, ranking as one of Asia's tiger economies if reforms are genuine and sustained. For multinationals, this could become one of the most attractive new market opportunities among global frontier markets for the next few decades. However, like with any new frontier market, the tremendous opportunities also come with a high level of political and economic risks, so it will almost certainly be a wild, wild ride in this frontier market!

Cambodia: out of the killing fields

During the US war against the North Vietnamese in the 1960s and early 1970s, Cambodia became the target for a massive bombing campaign by the US Air Force, as the US government attempted to prevent the Viet Cong from using Cambodia as a safe haven for mounting their operations. The increasing instability and intensive bombing of Cambodia helped to build support for a communist insurgency movement called the Khmer Rouge. After a civil war in Cambodia, the Khmer Rouge managed to seize control of the country. This was the beginning of one of the worst genocides in history, in which around 30 per cent of the Cambodian population would be killed.

An estimated 1.4 million people were murdered during the genocide that took place in Cambodia under the reign of terror of the Khmer Rouge from 1975 until 1978. Due to the effects of disease and starvation on the rest of the population as the economy disintegrated under the Khmer Rouge, the overall death toll during this period was in the range of 2.5 to 3 million, out of a total estimated population of 8 million prior to the genocide. UNICEF assessments place estimated deaths at the higher end of the range.

Large segments of the population were wiped out in a targeted way, particularly the Buddhist monks, who were seen as a threat to the regime, as well as the intelligentsia, including teachers, doctors and scientists. The Cambodian nation – its people and its economy – was essentially destroyed by the genocide perpetrated by the Khmer Rouge regime. The lunacy of the Khmer Rouge under their leader, Pol Pot, was also reflected in their concept of economic policy-making regarding the financial system. The great plan they conceived involved ending the banking system altogether, which they did in a rather melodramatic way, by actually blowing up the central bank and throwing all its currency reserves onto the roadside.

The downfall of the Khmer Rouge regime was eventually triggered only by their fear that their former allies, the Vietnamese, were seeking to dominate Cambodia as well. In a further extension of their insane visions of the future, the Khmer Rouge government actually attempted to attack the vastly superior Vietnamese forces. After ongoing border conflict for several years, the Vietnamese finally decided to end the conflict by invading Cambodia on Christmas Day 1978, and ousting the Khmer Rouge government led by their genocidal dictator Pol Pot. The Vietnamese, having crushed the Khmer Rouge forces, installed a pro-Vietnamese government and maintained a large military force in Cambodia to prevent further attempts to seize power by the Khmer Rouge, who had fled into exile.

The Vietnamese intervention in Cambodia drew a powerful reaction from China, which was a key backer of the Khmer Rouge regime. The Chinese Army invaded Vietnam on 17th February 1979, in a massive attack involving an estimated 200,000 troops and large formations of tanks. However, the Chinese were stunned by the capability of the battle-hardened Vietnamese troops, who inflicted heavy losses on them. Although the Chinese managed to gain significant ground, after a month of bitter fighting they withdrew back to their border, leaving the Vietnamese military still in control of Cambodia. While there are still no official estimates from either side of casualties, estimates of Chinese troops killed range as high as 25,000, indicating that there were very heavy casualties. With the bulk of the Vietnamese Army positioned to defend Hanoi and not even engaged yet with the Chinese Army, the Chinese withdrawal may have reflected a recognition that they would have been heavily defeated had they pressed further towards Hanoi. Vietnam also suffered heavy casualties according to most estimates, with the Chinese pursuing a scorched earth policy by destroying the areas they had captured. Nevertheless. the Vietnamese army further enhanced its reputation after stemming the Chinese invasion, having successfully fought three of the world's military powers, France, the US and China, within a relatively short timeframe.

In one of the most shameful episodes in the annals of Western democracy, the US and other major Western powers sided with China to back the Khmer Rouge government as the 'legitimate' government of Cambodia in the United Nations. This happened after they had committed genocide on their population and after they had been ousted by the Vietnamese armed forces. The Western powers continued to pursue the political isolation of Vietnam while Khmer Rouge leader Pol Pot, one of the world's most ruthless dictators, lived in Thailand, untouched by justice. He died in his sleep in 1998. He should have been hanged for crimes against humanity.

After the Vietnamese intervention, the long process of rehabilitation of the Cambodian economy began. The political rise of Hun Sen, who had been a Khmer Rouge soldier during the Cambodian civil war but had fled to Vietnam during the Khmer Rouge genocide, was rapid. He was appointed as Minister of Foreign Affairs under the new Vietnam-backed government of Cambodia, and eventually became prime minister in 1985.

An international negotiation process continued for years to find a lasting peace settlement for Cambodia to end the continuing guerrilla warfare still being conducted by elements of the Khmer Rouge against the Vietnam-backed Cambodian government. An agreement was finally reached in October 1991, under the terms of which the United Nations would establish a peacekeeping force in Cambodia, supervise a transition process to democratic elections and assist with large-scale resettlement of displaced refugees.

In 1993, after national elections, Hun Sen, who led the Cambodian People's Party, entered into a coalition government with Prince Ranariddh's FUNCINPEC Party, which had won 45.5 per cent of the total vote. However, Hun Sen eventually ousted his coalition partner in a coup in 1997 after violent clashes between supporters of the two parties. Since that time, he has remained the prime minister, albeit having had to work with coalition partnerships at various points, including having formed a new coalition government with the FUNCINPEC Party after the 1998 elections.

The Cambodian nation had to start again from the ground up in 1979, and even by 1999, it remained one of the poorest countries in the world, with the United Nations estimating that per capita GDP was only USD 300 per person in 1999. The process of economic development was very slow, due to the continued pursuit of communist approaches to economic management.

However, in the last decade, there have been clear signs that Cambodia is entering a more dynamic growth path, helped by the economic transition of its close political ally, Vietnam, away from communism as well as the rapid economic growth of China. Indeed, rising wage costs in coastal China have resulted in significant investment flows coming into Cambodia for establishing low-cost manufacturing operations for export, notably in the textiles and clothing sector. China had repaired its political relations with Cambodia following Hun Sen's coup in 1997, and the economic relationship between China and Cambodia has strengthened considerably since that time, with a strong flow of Chinese aid and investment financing for Cambodian public sector projects, as well as rapidly growing bilateral trade.

The discovery of oil and gas reserves in Cambodia has also resulted in the initial steps to developing oil production, which could also significantly contribute to economic development. Significant offshore oil and gas reserves in the Gulf of Thailand are the subject of a territorial dispute between Thailand and Cambodia, and if some settlement can eventually be found for this, then it is possible that significant further oil and gas production could be realised. Although the dispute has remained unresolved for three decades, there are some signs that negotiations could progress again to find some form of production-sharing agreement between the two countries.

The process of rebuilding Cambodia's financial sector has been slow, but the establishment of a new stock market in Phnom Penh has created new optimism about the potential for more rapid financial sector development. The government has taken steps towards privatising the state-owned enterprises (SOE) that control much of the Cambodian economy, and the first SOE privatisation on the new stock exchange took place in April 2012, when the Phnom Penh Water Supply Authority was part-privatised. The Cambodian government plans to undertake similar IPOs for other SOEs in the near future, which should help to make the fledgling stock exchange a more significant window for capital-raising by Cambodian companies.

Cambodia is also a member of ASEAN, and has commitments for trade liberalisation under the ASEAN Free Trade Area agreement, which should also contribute to the momentum for economic reforms.

The Cambodian economy has grown at a pace of around 6 per cent per year over 2010–12, and the IMF has estimated that its medium-term potential GDP growth rate is slightly above 7 per cent. Per capita GDP reached USD 900 per person in 2011, and is expected to move above USD 1,000 by 2012–13. While this still remains low by East Asian standards, it shows that significant progress has been achieved over the last decade. Importantly, Cambodia now appears to be on a sustained path of rapid economic growth, based on its key economic growth engines of agriculture, textiles exports and tourism. The ASEAN framework will also provide an important driver for continued economic reforms.

Mongolia's great mining boom

About twenty years ago, when Mongolia first began to liberalise its Soviet-style centrally planned economy, a development economist I knew visited the country to provide technical assistance. His anecdotal reports on the country were not particularly encouraging. Ulaanbaatar was then a drab grey town with little to do, and, worse still, during the long winter months the choice of food seemed to be restricted to mutton, goat meat and pickled vegetables. The accommodation for visitors was equally spartan.

Today, Ulaanbaatar is still a drab, grey, frontier mining town. The concept of public transport is pretty much nonexistent. There are some taxis, but these are few and far between. Despite the mining boom, average household incomes are still very low by international standards. Rough, tough Mongolians swill vodka and are ready to rob injudicious foreigners of their wallets if they stray out on their own at night.

However, times are changing rapidly. LVMH opened its first store in Ulaanbaatar in 2009. A Hilton hotel is under construction. Supermarkets offer a wide range of imported foods, and international restaurants are opening up.

What has changed to bring about this international investor interest? There were two fundamental drivers of change. Firstly, the liberalisation of Mongolia's economy included significant new legislation allowing foreign mining companies to develop Mongolian minerals, with discoveries of vast mineral wealth in Mongolia. Secondly, China's rapid economic development continued to drive demand for new sources of commodities, creating a ready market for Mongolia's mineral wealth.

Two major mineral projects are currently in the process of transforming Mongolia's economy. For Mongolia watchers, these are known as 'TT' and 'OT'.

TT is the abbreviation for Tavan Tolgoi, a vast coking coal deposit in the Gobi desert. Relatively low extraction costs and proximity to the Chinese border have made the development of these coal deposits highly attractive, with a ready Chinese market for the coking and thermal coal that can be exported from this project. Coking coal is needed for China's steel industry, which is forecast to grow significantly over the next decade. Thermal coal is needed for China's fast-growing energy demand.

OT is the abbreviation for Oyu Tolgoi, a world-class copper and gold project that is expected to become the third largest copper mine in the world once it reaches full production. This project is also located in the Gobi desert, around 110 kilometres away from Tavan Tolgoi.

These two projects are set to dramatically change the Mongolian economy. Mongolia has a very small population of around 2.8 million persons, with a GDP estimated at around USD 8 billion. However, the production and exports from TT and OT will result in very large increases in total Mongolian output. As a result of the development of TT's coal exports to China, Mongolia's annual coal exports are projected to rise from 28 million tons in 2012 to 130 million tons by 2025. Even over the next three years, the impact on Mongolian GDP will be very substantial, as TT coal production is expected to triple by 2015. Similarly, the commencement of OT production is expected to lift Mongolian GDP by 30 per cent over the period 2013–14. This is on the back of real GDP growth of 17 per cent in 2011.

This rapid growth in GDP and mineral exports will create very substantial increases in government revenue, but it also creates the high probability – almost a certainty – that Mongolia will experience the problems of what is known in economists jargon as 'Dutch disease'. The classic 'Dutch disease' cycle of events is that a large natural resources boom results in currency appreciation due to large export revenues, which reduces the competitiveness of other parts of the economy. This, in Mongolia's case, is of limited concern since other exports are relatively restricted. However, what seems inevitable is persistently high inflation due to strong growth in demand for labour and products in an economy with a limited labour supply, particularly for skilled workers. There is also a high risk that the large inflows of new fiscal revenue to the government will trigger fiscal largesse to maintain popular support for the government, adding to inflationary pressures.

Consequently, the mining boom also risks creating many severe macroeconomic problems for the Mongolian economy if not properly managed. One important safety value that other countries have used in such cases of large natural resources developments is to set aside a significant share of fiscal revenue in a sovereign wealth fund for future generations. This not only creates a long-term asset for future generations from a depleting natural resource, but also helps to mitigate the impact of the large boost to fiscal revenue and consequent inflationary risks if this is utilised to boost government consumption.

As the TT resources are owned by the state through Erdenes, the government has decided that all 2.7 million Mongolian citizens will be granted a share of the Erdenes Tavan Tolgoi project, with a total of 20 per cent of the Erdenes TT equity to be distributed in this way. However, this could well add to the Mongolian macroeconomic management problems, for if citizens decide to sell their shares after the project's IPO, there could be a significant boost to short-term consumer spending on top of the large expected increases in government spending.

However, Mongolia also needs massive infrastructure development to create transport infrastructure for its mining projects, as well as to develop essential infrastructure for its population, such as modern power stations, airports, hospitals and schools.

Therefore as fiscal revenue rises sharply over the medium term, a massive boom in infrastructure investment is also expected.

The Mongolian economy, therefore, is highly vulnerable to suffering from the problems of a mining boom and 'Dutch disease' over the next decade. Moreover, as its economy and exports will be almost entirely dependent on mineral exports, it will remain very vulnerable to global fluctuations in commodity prices as well as to the growth outlook for the Chinese economy. If China ever has a protracted hard landing, the great Mongolian mining boom can also turn into a great Mongolian mining bust, as has happened so often before with economies that are highly dependent on commodity exports.

Bangladesh – 'My Bengal of gold'

Amar shonar Bangla
Amar shonar Bangla
Ami tomake bhalobashi
Translation: My beloved Bengal, My Bengal of gold, I love you.
Opening verse of song by Rabindranath Tagore, Nobel Laureate for Literature 1913, adopted as Bangladesh national anthem in 1972.

Bangladesh is the world's seventh most populous country, with a population of around 142 million in 2010 – the fourth largest population in Asia. Like so many other Asian nations, its path to statehood was soaked in blood.

Bengal was the heart of British Imperial India, with British control over the territory of Bengal established and developed after the British East India Company and its troops defeated the army of the Bengali Nawab Siraj ud-Daulah at the Battle of Plassey in 1757. In 1772, the capital of British India became Calcutta, as British rule extended over the Indian subcontinent.

However, by 1905, the British viceroy, Lord Curzon, attempted to divide the province of Bengal into two along religious lines, with a Muslim East Bengal and a Hindu West Bengal. This provoked widespread political protests in Bengal, and it was at this time that Tagore wrote the song 'My Golden Bengal', as a key voice of opposition to the attempted partition. By 1911, the attempt at partition was abandoned. However, the seed of partition had been sown. When negotiations on Indian independence took place in 1946–47, the new nation of Pakistan that was created contained two geographically separate regions of West and East Pakistan, with East Bengal becoming East Pakistan.

The widespread communal violence that accompanied partition also took its bloody toll in Bengal, as Hindus and Muslims went through the horrors of separating their communities in a blood-bath. However, despite the many thousands of deaths during this violence, Bengal had experienced a greater human catastrophe in terms of the overall death toll just a few years earlier. In 1943, when British India was facing the threat of Japanese invasion and bitter battles were being fought in Burma, Bengal was experiencing a devastating famine.

The scale of the famine was vast, with the official famine commission established by the British government estimating that the death toll from famine and malnutrition was around 1.5 million persons, although some estimates are more than double this. There were multiple causes. In part, the Japanese occupation of Burma was a contributory factor, as Burma was a large rice-exporting state and had been an important source of rice imports for Bengal. However, there were also other contributory factors, including a poor rice harvest in Bengal combined with a devastating cyclone and accompanying tidal waves which had devastated low-lying areas. The refusal of the British government to recognise the severity of the famine was also a contributory factor, with a reluctance to ship grains from other regions or countries to alleviate the deprivation.

After the partition of India and Pakistan, East Bengal became part of Pakistan, with its own regional government. In 1955, the prime minister of East Bengal decided that the state would become East Pakistan. However, when Pakistani military dictator Ayub Khan took power in 1958, a long period of direct military rule began. Eventually, discontent with the economic situation in Pakistan became so great and civil unrest became so widespread during 1969 that Ayub Khan resigned and was replaced by Yahya Khan.

Yahya Khan promised a rapid return to constitutional government, and elections were held in 1970. In East Pakistan, the Bengal nationalist party, the Awami League, won a landslide victory, and their leader, Sheikh Mujibur Rahman, claimed an overall majority in the Pakistani National Assembly with 167 of the 300 directly elected seats. However, in West Pakistan the Pakistan People's Party led by Zulfikar Ali Bhutto had won the majority of seats in West Pakistan, so an impasse developed about how to form a government. After long negotiations no solution was found and on 1st March 1971, Yahya Khan decided to indefinitely postpone the commencement of the new National Assembly.

This triggered an outbreak of widespread civil unrest in East Pakistan, and the Pakistani Army in East Pakistan, under the command of General Tikka Khan, imposed a military crackdown in the East. Sheik Mujib was arrested and taken to West Pakistan, the Awami League was banned and Pakistani armed forces commenced a violent repression of the population of East Pakistan.

A Bengali major, Ziaur Rahman, with the support of Bengali political leaders from the Awami League, declared independence from Pakistan, forming the new independent nation of Bangladesh. The Bengali freedom fighter movement, the Mukti Bahini, was also formed, although it had a desperately unequal struggle against the powerful military forces of the Pakistani Army.

For months, the Pakistani forces under General Tikka Khan brutally suppressed the Bengali population. As with other episodes of genocide, there are no exact figures for the total number of people killed. A number of estimates made after careful research cluster around a figure of 300,000 people killed, although some estimates are as high as 1.5 million to 3 million deaths. An estimated 7 to 10 million Bengali refugees fled across the Indian border to escape the massacres.

Meanwhile, US President Nixon continued to give his strong support to the Pakistani Army. In a letter he wrote to General Yahya Khan during the Pakistani military action in Bangladesh, in which he thanked Yahya Khan for his help in building contacts with China, Nixon felt able to state the sentiments quoted below despite the information his own US government officials were sending about the genocide taking place in Bangladesh.

> Those who want a more peaceful world in the generation to come will forever be in your debt. Letter from US President Nixon to General Yahya Khan, 7th August 1971, The National Security Archive Electronic Briefing Book 79, George Washington University, December 2002.

When US State Department officials in Dhaka reported on the genocide in their cables, these were ignored, as the US government continued to support its alliance with the Pakistani military government at all costs.

Amongst the many cables from the US government officials on the ground indicating genocide, the most famous has become known as 'The Blood Telegram', signed by the US Consul General Archer Kent Blood and other US government officials from USAID and USIS stationed in Dhaka during the Pakistani military action in 1971. For his integrity, Archer Blood paid a high price. Blood, who had served in the Second World War as a US naval officer in the Pacific, was immediately recalled from his Consul General post in Dhaka back to the US. He was then sidelined in an administrative role in human resources, ostensibly in disgrace for his actions. However, the light of history shines brightly on those persons who acted with integrity and exposes those whose conduct should be held in disgrace over this matter.

'Our government has failed to denounce the suppression of democracy. Our government has failed to denounce atrocities. Our government has failed to take forceful measures to protect its citizens while at the same time bending over backwards to placate the West Pakistan-dominated government. Our government has evidenced what many will consider moral bankruptcy, ironically at a time when the U.S.S.R. sent President Yahya Khan a message defending democracy.'... 'But we have chosen not to intervene, even morally, on the grounds that the Awami conflict, in which unfortunately the overworked term genocide is applicable, is purely an internal matter of a sovereign state. Private Americans have expressed disgust. We, as professional civil servants, express our dissent with current policy and fervently hope that our true and lasting interests here can be defined and our policies redirected...'

The Blood Telegram, 6th April 1971: confidential telegram from American Consulate in Dacca to US Secretary of State on subject of 'Dissent from US Policy Toward East Pakistan'. Cable reclassified as 'Secret' by US State Department on 7th April 1971, The National Security Archive Electronic Briefing Book 79, George Washington University, December 2002.

Meanwhile, the Indian government had been supporting the Mukti Bahini, and tensions between Pakistan and India continued to escalate. On 3rd December 1971, Pakistan launched air strikes against Indian airbases, and the Indian military launched retaliatory strikes as well as a blitzkrieg campaign to liberate Bangladesh. Despite the US administration's efforts to prop up the

Pakistani military by arranging for the supply of fighter aircraft via third countries to work around a US embargo imposed by the US Congress on arms to Pakistan, as well as sending a US aircraft carrier into the Bay of Bengal, the Indian Army continued their rapid advance. After a 13-day campaign, Dhaka was liberated and the Pakistani forces in Bangladesh surrendered.

Since becoming a sovereign state, Bangladesh has faced considerable political unrest and instability, while its population has remained one of the poorest in the world. The low-lying floodplains in the Bay of Bengal are vulnerable to cyclones and tidal waves, which have periodically created tremendous destruction and loss of life. Bangladesh is one of the most vulnerable countries to the impact of global warming and rising sea levels, which creates tremendous economic, political and social challenges over the coming decades.

Yet Bangladesh in the last decade, despite a turbulent domestic political scene, has managed to achieve relatively consistent high growth, averaging around 5.8 per cent per year, helped by the competitiveness of its labour force for low-cost manufacturing, notably in the textiles and clothing industry. With wage costs rising in China, Bangladesh has benefited from rapid growth in textiles exports to key global markets including the US and EU. Around 4 million workers are employed in the fast-growing garment industry, with over three-quarters being women.

In addition, Bangladesh has substantial natural gas reserves, creating significant potential for development of these resources for both domestic consumption as well as exports. The recent resolution of a dispute over offshore territorial claims between Bangladesh and Myanmar was settled in an international court, which could allow this prospective area to be developed relatively soon.

One of the most impressive outcomes in Bangladesh's economic development over the last twenty years has been very substantial progress in human development. The share of the population in poverty has been halved since 1990, according to the UNDP and World Bank estimates, from around 60 per cent in 1990 to 32 per cent by 2010. The enrolment ratio of children in primary school education has risen from 61 per cent to 91 per cent over that same period.

Like other Asian frontier markets, there are still considerable risks and challenges facing investors. Political risk in Bangladesh remains high, with the turbulent domestic political landscape being a key risk for the outlook. The high level of corruption and poor standards of governance are also key risks.

After its tragic and violent history, there is new hope that Bangladesh could join the ranks of the more rapidly growing Asian economies, which could lift tens of millions out of poverty. Finally, Tagore's vision about a 'Golden Bengal' may be realised.

The impact of Asia's frontier economies

A detailed examination of the outlook for all of Asia's new frontier economies is beyond the scope of this book, since there are quite a few countries that could be included amongst these ranks. The new frontier economies in ASEAN include Vietnam, Myanmar, Laos and Cambodia. Outside of ASEAN, the new frontier economies of Asia include Sri Lanka, Mongolia and Bangladesh. There are also other countries in Asia that could be included, such as Pakistan, due to its future potential as a manufacturing hub, and Papua New Guinea, due to its mineral and agricultural resources. The oil-rich Central Asian economies, such as Kazakhstan, could also be included in this list.

However, the key message from the overall perspective of their role in the future Asian economic landscape is that Asian frontier economies do have some of the most exciting economic growth prospects amongst the over 200-plus sovereign states worldwide.

Moreover, their potential impact is significant. Even if only the seven Asian frontier economies listed in table 9.1 are considered, these have a total population of over 300 million, which is significantly greater than the population of Indonesia. Their total GDP is around USD 375 billion, similar in total size of GDP to South Africa, which is now considered to be one of the BRIC economies.

Table 9.1 Asian frontier economies: the league table

	Size of GDP, 2011 USD billion	Size of Population million	GDP Growth Rate, 2011 annual % change
Bangladesh	113.0	142.3	6.1
Vietnam	122.7	87.8	5.9
Sri Lanka	59.1	20.7	8.2
Myanmar	51.9	50.0	5.5
Cambodia	12.9	13.4	6.1
Laos	7.9	6.5	8.3
Mongolia	8.5	2.7	17.3

Sources: IMF; government statistics.

Even though average GDP per capita remains very low in these seven frontier economies, the growth outlook for these countries as a group over the medium term averages around 6 per cent per year, which is roughly equivalent to Indonesia's medium term growth outlook. In effect, the grouping of these seven Asian frontier economies together comprise a total population and GDP size that is equivalent to another rising BRIC economy. This has the potential to significantly add to the growth momentum of the Asian region over the next decade.

However, all of these countries have significant risks and vulnerabilities, ranging from macroeconomic to political and operational risks. Weak governance, high levels of corruption, poorly developed regulatory systems and a lack of infrastructure are among the hurdles these countries face. The extent of political risk does vary significantly, but nevertheless is clearly very high in Myanmar, Sri Lanka and Bangladesh.

In the days of the Wild West in the 19th century, there was a frontier saying that 'there is no law west of the Pecos River'. The same is probably applicable for much of the territory in Asia's new frontiers.

The Wild, Wild East remains speculative territory but these countries also are Asia's new frontiers of considerable opportunity, with the potential for rapid economic growth over the long term. For those individuals and firms who are willing to accept high risks, there is the lure of adventure in the last remaining frontier economies of Asia as well as the opportunity to get high rewards.

Chapter 10

Future Asia

Conflict or cooperation?

War is not merely a political act, but also a real political instrument, a continuation of political commerce, a carrying out of the same by other means.

General Carl von Clausewitz, 'On War' ('Vom Kriege'),
Dummlers Verlag, Berlin, 1832, from the
English translation by Colonel J.J. Graham, 1874.
The Project Gutenberg eBook of 'On War'.

Battlegrounds of the future

Despite decades of economic progress and rising intra-Asian trade and investment, there are still significant fault lines for conflict in Asia. The scars of past wars also still run deep in many places, with national sentiment easily inflamed.

With China's economy set to become the largest in the world within a decade, there is considerable concern amongst some other Asian countries about the implications for China's military capability. Clearly the Chinese military will continue to grow significantly in size so long as the Chinese economy can deliver economic growth rates of around 7 to 8 per cent per year.

Given China's history of military tensions with a number of its neighbours, the rising military capability of China is increasing regional security concerns. China has uneasy relations with some of its ASEAN neighbours over disputed claims in the South China Sea, with potential oil and gas resources as well as control over maritime shipping lanes at stake. Recent confrontations have occurred between China and Vietnam as well as between China and the Philippines over disputed territorial claims. Given the fierce war between China and Vietnam in 1979, when Chinese forces invaded Vietnam, there are deep-seated concerns in Vietnam about China's growing military power.

Although tensions have eased considerably between China and Taiwan since the 1995–96 Taiwan Strait Crisis when the Chinese military launched missiles in the vicinity of the Taiwan Strait and undertook naval and amphibious landing exercises, the incident continues to serve as a stark reminder of the potential fault lines that still exist in the Taiwan Strait.

Long-smouldering tensions between China and Japan sparked into fresh flames in the summer of 2012, following the decision by the Japanese government to buy some islets that were under private Japanese ownership which are the subject of a territorial claim by China. The purchase of these islets, known as the Senkaku islands in Japan and as the Diaoyu islands in China, triggered a wave of anti-Japanese demonstrations and violent attacks on Japanese factories as well as Japanese citizens in China. Japanese branded products, such as autos, were also attacked by enraged Chinese rioters. Military tensions also escalated, with China having sent a fleet of armed surveillance ships into waters nearby the islands. Taiwan, which also claims the islands, sent a fleet of fishing vessels supported by coast guard ships to the area, and Japanese and Taiwanese coast guard vessels clashed with water cannon.

With China having become Japan's largest export market, and bilateral trade between the two nations reaching USD 345 billion in 2011, the economic impact of protracted anti-Japanese sentiment in China could have significant adverse consequences for the economies of both nations. Immediately following the attacks, there were significant cancellations of Japanese travel bookings to China, resulting in Japanese airlines reducing flights to Chinese cities.

With China having been the destination for large-scale Japanese investment in a wide range of manufacturing industries for decades, such anti-Japanese sentiment could trigger a shift in Japanese investment in manufacturing to other low-cost manufacturing hubs such as India, Thailand, Vietnam and Mexico, to reduce the vulnerability of their global supply chain to such events being repeated in China. Large multinationals from Europe and North America may also review their vulnerability to such political uncertainty and civil unrest in China, and could decide to protect their global supply chains by reducing their reliance on Chinese-sourced production and investing in new plants in other competitive emerging markets.

Beyond the significant economic consequences of such tensions, maritime confrontations between Chinese and Japanese vessels could create significant risks of escalating tensions and even conflict.

On its border with India, China also has fraught relations due to disputed territorial claims over the regions of Aksai Chin and Arunachal Pradesh. A border war was fought between China and India in 1962, which has continued to be a memory that has haunted India as its military forces were heavily defeated. With the border dispute still unresolved, India continues to fear the military threat from China, even though bilateral economic relations have developed strongly over the past decade.

One of the major geopolitical risks in Asia is the very difficult political relationship between India and Pakistan, given the number of wars that have been fought between these countries since they were granted independence from British rule in 1947. It is hard to be very optimistic about the future of bilateral relations between India and Pakistan despite the efforts of both governments at various times to build confidence and improve relations. The unresolved issue of Kashmir still remains a key difference between the countries. It seems unlikely that both sides will come to any solution soon about this, given public opinion in both countries, although the Indian and Pakistani governments have held talks to establish a framework for settling the Kashmir dispute.

A key threat to the peace process continues to come from terrorist attacks on India which are somehow linked to Pakistani-based terrorist groups, even though these do not have any involvement or support from the Pakistani government. The impact such attacks have on public opinion in India could at some point force a limited Indian military response which, although it may be directed at terrorist training camps in Pakistan, could provoke an escalating response by the Pakistani military and trigger a serious conflict.

Therefore, tensions between India and Pakistan are likely to remain one of the key geopolitical flashpoints in the Asia-Pacific for the foreseeable future. The nuclear weapons capability of both sides continues to make this one of the key threats to global security in the 21st century.

The Korean peninsula is another major geopolitical flashpoint in the Asia-Pacific, with North Korea also having some nuclear weapons. At present, it seems that the North Korean regime is continuing to pursue the old policies of nuclear blackmail that were utilised by Kim Jong II. South Korea faces considerable contingent fiscal liabilities to pay for unification with the North, so it may prefer to see a more gradualist solution with a protracted transition period for North Korea to converge towards the South Korean economy rather than a sudden unification process occurring.

An Asian arms race?

With significant geopolitical risks still affecting the Asian security landscape, there is a very real possibility that the combination of rapid Asian economic growth overlaid on a landscape of political fault lines will trigger an arms race in the Asia-Pacific. Indeed, there are troubling signs that this has already begun.

At the heart of East Asian concerns are the implications for Chinese defence spending due to the economic ascent of China towards becoming the world's largest economy. The fear is that China's rapid economic growth will continue to translate into very significant increases in Chinese military expenditure, creating an asymmetric military balance of power in Asia-Pacific dominated by China. The US Department of Defense estimated that total Chinese military-related spending in 2011 ranged between USD 120 billion and USD 180 billion, with an 11.2 per cent increase in the Chinese defence budget announced for 2012.

Given China's recent history of military invasions into India in 1962 and Vietnam in 1979, two of China's neighbours have reasons to fear a Chinese military build-up. In addition, despite the reduction of cross-Strait tensions between China and Taiwan in the recent past, Taiwan has continuously been in a state of military preparedness for a Chinese invasion. The Philippines has also become involved in a dispute with China over territorial claims in the South China Sea, with a protracted standoff between Chinese vessels and ships from the Philippines in the waters off Scarborough Shoal in 2012.

The initial signs of the development of a blue water capability in the Chinese navy are also contributing to regional concerns. China's first aircraft carrier has completed its sea trials. This ship is a redeveloped Russian aircraft carrier, and it is believed to be mainly intended for training purposes so that fighter pilots can learn to operate from an aircraft carrier, given China has never had any carriers before. However, the 2012 Pentagon Report to the US Congress on Chinese military capability assessed that China may already have commenced building its first indigenous aircraft carrier and have an operational blue water capability after 2015 with the intention of building multiple aircraft carriers.

Other Asian nations are also developing their naval capabilities. India has purchased an old Russian aircraft carrier, which is being redeveloped in Russia and is due to be delivered at the end of 2012 after substantial delays and cost overruns. Meanwhile, India is also building its own indigenous aircraft carriers, with the first of these already under construction and expected to become operational after 2015.

The Indian military relationship with Russia and heavy reliance on Russian military hardware has deep roots, born out of a lack of trust in the political and military relationship with the US. The US political and military support for Pakistan during the 1965 and 1971 Indo-Pak wars are not easily forgotten, whereas Russia has been dependable politically and militarily whenever India has faced a conflict. While the US military relationship with India was boosted considerably when President Kennedy provided military equipment to India after the Chinese border war in 1962, the subsequent wars with Pakistan highlighted to India that the US was strongly aligned with Pakistan politically and militarily. The contrast was stark.

In December 1962, a memorandum from the US Joints Chiefs of Staff stated that:

"US interests in the Indian situation require that a degree of material assistance be rendered to meet Indian demands for air defense support."
Memorandum from the US Joint Chiefs of Staff to Secretary of Defense McNamara
December 14th, 1962
Source: Foreign Relations of the US, 1961–1963, Vol. XIX, South Asia, Document 225, US State Department Historical Documents

On the ground, this translated into round-the-clock airlifting of supplies to the Indian army. Indeed, the US 40th Airlift Squadron had already deployed a squadron of C-130 transports to India during the conflict, conducting an airlift of critical military supplies to the Indian troops in the Himalayas. This airlift operation in India by the US Air Force continued for over one year.

However, by 1971, during the Indo-Pak war over Pakistan's occupation of Bangladesh, the position of the Nixon Administration severely damaged the relationship with India. President Nixon actually despatched an aircraft carrier task force from the US Seventh Fleet, as a threat to try to stop the Indian armed forces from completely destroying the Pakistani military. In a conversation with the Chinese Ambassador to the United Nations, Kissinger, as Assistant to the President for National Security Affairs, is quoted in US State Department records as stating:

"In addition, we are moving a number of naval ships in the West Pacific to the Indian Ocean: an aircraft carrier accompanied by four destroyers and a tanker, and a helicopter carrier and two destroyers."

"...if the People's Republic were to consider the situation on the Indian subcontinent a threat to its security, and if it took measures to protect its security, the US would oppose efforts of others to interfere with the People's Republic."

"...So it seems to us that through a combination of pressure and political moves it is important to keep India from attacking in the West, to gain time to get more arms into Pakistan and to restore the situation."

Memorandum of Conversation, New York, December 10th 1971 between Ambassador Huang Hua, PRC Permanent Representative to the UN and Henry Kissinger Foreign Relations of the US, US State Department Historical Documents Vol XI, Document 274

It took many years for successive US administrations under President Bill Clinton and later President George W. Bush to gradually begin to rebuild the military ties between the US and India, which have resulted in some thawing of the bilateral military relationship and limited Indian military purchases from the US.

Vietnam, which has also had territorial disputes with China in the South China Sea, faced an escalating situation in 2011 when Chinese naval patrol boats confronted a Vietnamese oil and gas exploration ship. Vietnam has ordered six Kilo Class attack submarines from Russia, as well as twenty Su-30MK2V fighters, in order to upgrade its ageing military capabilities, with reports of negotiations for the acquisition of additional Su-30 fighters. After the long history of bitter enmity between Vietnam and the US over the Vietnam War and its legacy, Vietnam's political and military ties with the US may begin to thaw as Vietnam attempts to deal with China over the South China Sea territorial dispute.

Even the Philippines, which had no fighter jets in its air force, has announced that it intends to buy jet fighter trainers from South Korea, presumably as a preparatory step to building its own operational air force.

Other Asian countries are also upgrading their air forces, with Japan having decided to purchase forty-two Lockheed Martin F-35A Lightning II JSAF stealth fighters, while India announced that the French company Dassault's 'Rafale' fighter is the preferred bidder at the final stage of negotiations for India's Medium Multirole Combat Aircraft (MMRCA) competition for one hundred and twenty-six aircrafts. Meanwhile, Indonesia intends to expand its fighter squadrons from seven to twelve, increasing its existing fleet of Su-30MK2 fighters and US F-16s with additional orders for new aircrafts of each type.

Consequently, rapid economic growth in the Asia-Pacific is also being reflected in significant military spending, partly in response to anxieties about China's own rapidly growing military capacity. Whether this arms race accelerates further will reflect the abilities of Asian countries to develop a new framework for greater security dialogue that can effectively serve to reduce the risk of conflict in the Asia-Pacific.

Resource wars

Another dimension of national security concerns in the Asia-Pacific centre around resource security. China and India, in particular, face significantly increasing demand for energy imports over the long-term, based on their rapid economic growth rates and large populations of around 1.2 billion persons in each country.

For both China and India, the acquisition of international energy assets to try to improve energy security has become a key objective, with state-owned oil companies in both countries having embarked on programmes to acquire international oil and gas assets worldwide. Another dimension of energy security is to ensure the integrity of shipping lanes to permit the steady delivery of oil and gas shipments, and this is reflected in ambitious expansion programmes by both the Chinese and Indian navies.

However, the efforts by Asian commodity-importing nations to secure strategic commodity assets abroad has also triggered resource nationalism in some countries, including Indonesia and Mongolia. In Mongolia, the announcement that Aluminium Corporation of China (CHALCO) would buy a controlling stake in Mongolian mining company SouthGobi Resources, a coking coal miner, has triggered new proposed legislation in parliament to prevent such strategic acquisitions of Mongolian resource assets by foreign state-owned companies. The CHALCO bid was subsequently abandoned.

Similarly, Indonesia has changed its mining ownership laws in 2012 to ensure that a 51 per cent stake of all Indonesian mining operations are controlled by Indonesian interests, with foreign firms that already own mining assets in Indonesia given a number of years to adjust down their ownership stakes to comply with the new law. Furthermore, the Indonesian government has also introduced a new export tax on unprocessed exports of fourteen mineral commodities, in order to encourage greater value-adding in the domestic economy.

Indonesia, which used to be a member of the Organisation of Petroleum Exporting Countries (OPEC), is also facing its own energy security challenges due to declining production of oil amidst rising domestic energy demand. Consequently, Indonesia is no longer a net oil exporting country, and in the future its oil imports may rise significantly unless new domestic discoveries meet the incremental demand.

Even Indonesian LNG (Liquefied Natural Gas) exports, which used to be the largest in the world, are now facing constraints due to rapidly rising domestic demand for gas. Indonesia is consequently phasing out its LNG export contracts as they come up for renewal, while LNG import terminals are being built.

Similarly, Myanmar has decided that it will not export additional gas from its gas fields, as it intends to retain the gas for domestic consumption and to support the energy requirements of the domestic industry.

Consequently, the rapid economic growth of emerging Asia is creating resource security issues in a number of areas, including energy, minerals as well as agricultural commodities. Another area of resource security concerns are water resources.

A US Intelligence Community assessment released in 2012 has identified water problems, including water shortages, flooding and poor water quality, as key risks for social instability and disruptions over the next ten years in many developing country regions, including Asia-Pacific. The problems of South Asia are highlighted, particularly due to the dependence of hundreds of millions of people on the glacial meltwaters from the Hindu Kush and Himalayas.

The competition amongst Asian nations for scarce resources such as oil and gas, water as well as fisheries have the potential to add further tensions and disputes to existing regional fault lines and conflicts.

Building cooperation and conflict resolution in Asia

The Asia-Pacific region is increasingly becoming the centre of gravity for the world economy as China, India and ASEAN have emerged as key engines for global economic growth. However, Asia continues to face significant challenges to maintaining peace and stability in the region.

Although ASEAN has achieved a great deal in terms of regional economic and trade cooperation, there are ongoing political tensions that create potential fault lines. These include the disputed land border between Cambodia and Thailand around the Preah Vihear Temple and disputed offshore territorial claims over oil and gas reserves in the Gulf of Thailand, and the tensions amongst Asian littoral states in the South China Sea over disputed territorial claims relating to offshore oil and gas resources.

Despite these disputes, there is considerable scope for optimism that ASEAN can form the hub for regional security dialogue, most notably reflected in the recent achievements of a number of ASEAN countries in combating piracy in the Straits of Malacca through close cooperation and coordination amongst their governments and military forces.

Risks to regional security

As the economic power of the Asia-Pacific region continues to grow, the sustained rapid growth in GDP of many Asian economies gives greater scope for sustained growth in government expenditures, including defence. As the military capabilities of Asia-Pacific countries continue to rise, the need for strengthening regional dialogue on peace and security becomes increasingly important, to ensure that the fruits of industrialisation and economic development are not dissipated by conflict, as occurred in Europe during the First and Second World Wars.

While the Asia-Pacific region has managed to avoid major regional conflicts for an extended period of time, there are many existing political fault lines and flashpoints that remain major risks for regional peace and security. Apart from the territorial disputes in the South China Sea, other Asian flashpoints include long-standing Indo-Pak border tensions and military tensions in the Korean peninsula, with the latter having reached crisis point during 2010 following the Cheonan incident and the shelling of Yeonpyeong Island.

In coming decades, the Asia-Pacific region will also face growing new challenges from the impact of climate change, which will put new pressures on key resources such as land and water, creating additional potential fault lines for regional tensions. Therefore, the need for establishing strong regional mechanisms for dialogue on peace and security has become increasingly pressing.

The existing disputes over offshore territorial claims in the South China Sea and Gulf of Thailand reflect growing concerns about resource security as the energy needs of the rapidly growing Asian economies expand, particularly as rapidly growing global demand for oil and gas and constraints on development of low-cost new sources of supply is putting upward pressure on oil prices over the long-term. Consequently, unless mechanisms are found for peaceful resolution of these disputes, there is a significant risk that these resource-related disputes could become a flashpoint for future military tensions amongst involved countries.

Mechanisms for dialogue

One of the key existing forums for regional security dialogue is the Shangri-La Dialogue (SLD), a major annual mechanism for regional discussions that has been taking place for a decade. At the SLD held in Singapore on 3–5 June 2011, a key focus for many of the regional defence ministers attending was to discuss the scope for strengthening dialogue amongst Asia-Pacific countries. Malaysian Prime Minister Najib Razak specifically identified the new ASEAN Defence Ministers Plus with Eight Dialogue Partners forum (ADMM+), which was established by ASEAN in October 2010, and the ASEAN Regional Forum (ARF), as key platforms for regional dialogue on defence and security.

The ADMM+ process has already made significant progress, with the establishment of Expert Working Groups under the auspices of the ASEAN Defence Senior Officials' Meeting Plus. The five expert groups are in:

- Humanitarian Assistance and Disaster Relief
- Maritime Security
- Peacekeeping Operations
- Military Medicine
- Counter-terrorism

These working groups will offer mechanisms for rapid implementation of new measures to improve cooperation in these key areas. For example, given the succession of major natural disasters that have afflicted the Asia-Pacific in recent years, including the Indian Ocean tsunami, the major flooding of Myanmar and the Japanese earthquake and tsunami in 2011, the importance of greater cooperation in humanitarian assistance and disaster relief is one very important and practical priority for the Asia-Pacific region, given the considerable logistical difficulties in relief operations that have been evident in such catastrophic events.

As China is already the largest economy in the Asia-Pacific and is expected to become the world's largest economy within a decade, any regional security dialogue would need to have the full support and cooperation of China. At the Shangri-La Dialogue on 5th June 2011, the Chinese Minister of National Defense made a strong statement in favour of regional multilateral security dialogues and cooperation mechanisms.

"ADMM+ is the official cooperation mechanism of seniormost cooperation and widest participation in the Asia-Pacific region." ... "What's more, the recent ASEAN Defence Senior Officials' Meeting Plus has officially approved Expert Working Groups in the five identified areas. Practical cooperation is now ready to go. I'm confident that as countries in this region work together, security cooperation in the Asia-Pacific will have a bright future." (General Liang Guanglie, Minister of National Defense and Member of the Central Military Commission, China. IISS Shangri-La Dialogue, 5th June 2011)

The development of regional security dialogue through the ADMM+ forum has also been strongly supported by India; Asia's other rapidly emerging BRIC economy. India remains one of the key geopolitical flashpoints for regional conflict, due to disputed borders with two other nuclear powers, Pakistan and China.

India lauds the initiatives of the ASEAN countries in setting up fora like the ARF and the ADMM+ which provide the basis on which we can forge a framework under which countries of this region can come together to build mutual confidence and consensus, as we look for solutions to our common problems. (M.M. Pallam Raju, Minister of State for Defence, India. IISS Shangri-La Dialogue, 5th June 2011)

One example of the positive achievements of closer regional cooperation is the substantial reduction in piracy in the Straits of Malacca, through which 74,000 vessels pass each year and which is also a key shipping lane for oil supplies for East Asia, handling around 25 per cent of all global oil shipments, equivalent to around 11 million barrels of oil per day, according to the Marine Department Malaysia. Singapore, Malaysia, Indonesia and Thailand have been working together in the Straits to reduce piracy, and in 2010, the International Maritime Bureau reported that piracy incidents in the Straits had been virtually eliminated. This reflects a number of joint initiatives involving naval patrols, aerial surveillance and intelligence sharing.

This example demonstrates what can be achieved through close regional security cooperation to combat a problem that had been persistent and substantial historically, and was still a major threat to shipping less than a decade ago.

Prospects for cooperation

The Asia-Pacific region is becoming the new centre of global economic power in the 21st century. In order to ensure sustained peaceful economic development and industrialisation, accompanied by poverty reduction and improving standards of living, it is a key priority for Asian countries to establish strong mechanisms to promote peace and security in the Asia-Pacific region.

This is important not only to address existing border disputes that currently remain unresolved in a number of Asian countries, but also to create dialogue mechanisms to address new emerging challenges to Asia-Pacific security, such as climate change, transnational crime and resource security issues.

There is increasing momentum and consensus amongst the key Asia-Pacific countries that ASEAN can play the key role and provide a platform for dialogue for enhancing regional peace and cooperation, using the existing ARF and ADMM+ mechanisms, augmented by the Shangri-La Dialogue, to build regional peace and security.

In order for such dialogue mechanisms to be effective, the dialogue partners need to include key nations from the Asia-Pacific beyond the ASEAN membership, such as Japan, China, South Korea and India. This will provide a new architecture for defence and security cooperation, to complement the existing mechanisms for economic and financial cooperation such as the ASEAN+3 Chiang Mai Initiative.

Establishing a regular dialogue process and dispute resolution mechanism may offer the best chance to avert the risks of future conflict in the Asia-Pacific. The devastating human costs of the Second World War in the Asia-Pacific theatre serve as a stark reminder of the potential consequences if Asian nations fail to establish a strong architecture for conflict prevention and resolution in the region.

Conclusion

The four engines of Asian growth

The four engines of Asian growth

The 21st century is the 'Asian Century'. The global economy is experiencing a fundamental rebalancing as emerging Asian economies experience sustained rapid growth. There are four main growth engines within Asia that will continue to support this Asian ascendancy during the 21st century.

Firstly, China has become the key driver of Asia's rapid economic growth and, although the Chinese economy will experience the fluctuations of the business cycle, its long-term growth rate over the next two decades is still expected to be an important supporting force for rapid expansion of economic growth, trade and investment within the Asia-Pacific region. China is expected to become the world's largest economy in around ten years' time. This will make China the single most important export market for most Asian countries.

Secondly, India is projected to overtake Japan in around fifteen years' time in terms of overall size of GDP in nominal terms. While the size of the Indian economy will be considerably smaller than that of China, nevertheless India will become an increasingly important force for Asian regional growth, as its trade and investment relationships with other Asian economies grow rapidly.

Asia's third force will be Indonesia, which should be considered in the same terms as the four BRIC economies, which are China, India, Russia and Brazil. It is one of the world's largest emerging markets and its GDP is expected to pass the USD one trillion threshold by 2015. With a population of 240 million and a fast-growing middle class, Indonesia has the potential to sustain real GDP growth of around 6 per cent per year. With significant infrastructure investment to reduce bottlenecks, Indonesia's average economic growth rate could even edge higher.

A fourth growth engine will be the agglomeration of Asia's next new frontier economies combined with the rest of the ASEAN economies.

Asia's fourth growth engine

While the first three growth engines of the Asia-Pacific are more clearly understood because each of them is a large individual economy, the fourth growth engine is less well recognised as it comprises a number of different Asian countries, all of which share the common characteristic of being fast-growing.

The first group of countries that are part of this fourth growth engine are a grouping of seven new frontier countries in Asia, comprising Bangladesh, Vietnam, Cambodia, Laos, Myanmar, Sri Lanka and Mongolia. These countries had a combined GDP of around USD 375 billion in 2011. This is the GDP equivalent of one of the world's larger emerging markets, South Africa, but all have been growing considerably faster than South Africa in the recent past. These Asian new frontier countries are showing the potential to achieve strong growth over the long-term, albeit some will inevitably suffer from macroeconomic imbalances and business cycle volatility in GDP growth as well as potential economic consequences of adverse political developments.

The second major group of countries that are part of this fourth growth engine are the ASEAN Trillion Dollar economies of Malaysia, Thailand and the Philippines, which are each projected to have USD GDP exceeding USD 1 trillion by 2030. Each of these countries has the capacity for sustained average long-term growth of 5 to 6 per cent per year.

In addition, the advanced economy of Singapore forms part of this fourth growth engine, due to its sustained strong average rate of economic growth.

The total size of ASEAN economies excluding Indonesia was USD 1.3 trillion in 2011. When the non-ASEAN frontier economies of Bangladesh, Sri Lanka and Mongolia are included, the total size of the GDP of this fourth Asian growth engine was USD 1.5 trillion in 2011. This was about the same as Australian GDP in 2011, and was not much lower than the GDP of India.

This fourth growth engine comprises a mixture of economies at different stages of economic development, but all have the potential for sustained, strong, long-term economic growth over the next two decades.

In Malaysia, the government has already laid out its Economic Transformation Plan for achieving annual average GDP growth of around 6 per cent per year over the next decade and becoming an advanced nation with a per capita GDP that is ranked among

Table C.1   Asia's fourth growth engine (size of
GDP, USD billion, 2011)

Asian Frontier Markets	375
ASEAN Trillion Dollar Countries	865
Singapore	260
Total Size	1,480

Source: IMF Statistics.

the high income economies. This strategy will be driven by the development of high value adding industries, notably service sector industries such as financial services, health care, education and tourism.

Thailand is also expected to become an economy with a total GDP exceeding USD 1 trillion by 2030. It is already ranked at number 17 globally in the World Bank's 2012 Ease of Doing Business ranking of 183 countries. It is already a middle-income nation, and with a strong competitive advantage in agricultural exports as well as in key manufacturing industries such as autos, electronics and chemicals, Thailand is well positioned for sustained strong growth.

The Philippines has suffered from weak governance and corruption for decades, but there are signs of a more dynamic economy emerging. The Business Processing Association of the Philippines reported that in 2011 revenues from the information technology and business process outsourcing industry grew by 24 per cent to reach total revenues of USD 11 billion, while employment rose 22 per cent to reach 638,000. The sector already accounts for 5 per cent of GDP, and the Association has projected annual industry growth of 15 per cent per year over the medium term, with the potential to generate 1.5 million new jobs by 2016. Meanwhile large flows of remittances from Filipino workers abroad continue to provide strong underpinning for domestic demand and the balance of payments, reaching USD 20 billion in 2011, or around 10 per cent of GDP. With medium term potential growth of around 5 per cent per year, the sustained reduction in government debt levels as a share of GDP could eventually give room for greater infrastructure development, and could boost long-term potential growth rates.

Singapore will remain one of the world's star economies, based on its strong competitive advantage as a knowledge hub, a top global international financial centre and a regional logistics hub. Despite already being a high-income economy with per capita

GDP comparable to the US, it is expected to sustain strong annual growth rates over the long term, pushing its total GDP close to the USD 1 trillion mark by 2030.

Most of the countries comprising Asia's fourth growth engine are well positioned to benefit from strong trade and investment flows with China, India and Indonesia, as well as sustained strong growth from domestic demand in the more populous countries such as Bangladesh and Vietnam.

The rise of emerging Asian consumers and multinationals

The four growth engines for the Asia-Pacific region will generate rapid growth in household incomes and consumer spending in the Asia-Pacific region, as the ranks of the Asian middle class grow rapidly. This will result in emerging Asia replacing the OECD economies as the key contributor to global consumer demand growth over the next three decades.

For multinationals worldwide facing increasing headwinds in the mature markets of the OECD, this is creating a new gold rush in the East. Rapid growth in demand is already evident in emerging Asia across a wide spectrum of products, including automobiles, household goods, luxury goods and key service industries such as banking and insurance products. There are also tremendous infrastructure requirements in emerging Asia, with an estimated USD 7 to 8 trillion of new infrastructure spending required in Asia over the next decade.

Urbanisation and the growth of emerging Asian cities is another important structural trend that will create vast opportunities for companies related to urban infrastructure development, as well as residential and commercial construction projects. The development of smart cities that are globally competitive will be a key priority for many emerging Asian countries, as regions compete to attract companies and create employment growth in the high value-adding industries of the knowledge economy.

The environmental and resource challenges facing developing Asian countries will also require massive investment in infrastructure, creating major opportunities for global construction companies. Many large Asian cities, including Mumbai, Jakarta and Bangkok, confront an urgent task to mitigate risks of large-scale flooding, while large urban as well as rural areas of Bangladesh,

Vietnam and other South-east Asian countries are vulnerable to rising sea levels due to global warming. Overall, infrastructure development will be a key priority for developing Asian governments for decades, and Asian infrastructure construction spending growth will be strong over the long-term.

However, multinationals from the OECD competing for business in Asia are also facing a very competitive corporate landscape, as increasing numbers of emerging market multinationals become substantial global players in a wide array of industries. As China overtakes the US to become the world's largest economy, the size of its largest companies will also increase, with corporate revenues and assets of these companies becoming very significant by international standards. This is already evident in the rankings of the world's largest companies, with a significant number of Chinese multinationals having entered the ranks of the world's 500 largest companies over the last decade.

As these Chinese multinationals continue to globalise and develop global footprints, their international expansion and mergers and acquisitions activities may create significant shockwaves amongst global competitors, as well as potentially creating a public backlash in some countries. There are already some signals of greater resource nationalism in some countries in response to fears about the scale of Chinese acquisitions of natural resource assets.

The rise of Asian emerging market multinationals will be led by Chinese firms, but other Asian countries will also have a significant number of large multinationals competing globally, including India, South Korea, Malaysia, Singapore and Indonesia. This will result in intensifying competition as established leading multinationals from the OECD face challenges from emerging market multinationals in key areas such as R&D and technological leadership, and rising mergers and acquisitions by emerging market firms to build market share.

In the construction and infrastructure sector, while there will be very strong growth in construction spending in long-term, competition is also increasingly fierce. Large Japanese, Chinese and South Korean construction companies compete intensely with US and European firms for Asian construction projects. Other Asian countries are also developing their capabilities in this segment, with Malaysia, Indonesia and India having fast-growing construction firms that are increasingly competing not just in their home market but in the rest of Asia as well as the Middle East.

While the prospects for sustained strong growth in the Asia-Pacific remain very favourable, the economic development challenges are large in many Asian countries. Moreover, the institutional and governance standards are often weak, with high levels of corruption, inadequate and ineffective national institutions, and difficult business climates in terms of the ease of doing business.

For other regions of the world, this rapid growth in Asia will also provide new growth opportunities for their own economies. South-South trade amongst developing countries is already growing rapidly, but will be further supported by demand for oil and gas, metals and agricultural commodities from the fast-growing Asian region. This will continue to gradually shift the structure of world trade towards greater diversification, reducing the vulnerability of developing countries to the business cycle in the US and EU.

The greater diversification of global markets away from the past overreliance on OECD consumer demand should also be beneficial for the EU and Japan, which are both facing weak domestic demand conditions for a protracted period. For European multinationals, which been heavily focused on EU trade, corporate strategies will increasingly shift towards tapping Asian markets and building commercial ties with Asia.

The new financial and economic architecture

As Asian economies such as China, India and Indonesia become increasingly key players on the geopolitical stage, the construction of the global financial and economic architecture will also need to evolve. The old Bretton Woods structure whereby the International Monetary Fund and World Bank were dominated by the US and Europe in terms of leadership as well as total voting rights will increasingly face pressure for more substantial changes in voting rights than have occurred so far.

The concept that someone from the US should always be the head of the World Bank and someone from Europe should lead the IMF has become an increasingly barbarous relic of the age of colonialism. It will be interesting to see how the hypocrisy on this issue develops once China becomes the world's largest economy. The logical extension of the current system would be that eventually China would have the largest number of voting rights in the IMF and World Bank, and that the head of the World Bank should always be Chinese.

The rising economic weight of the Asian region in the global economy over coming decades will demand that Asian countries will need to play a greater role in international governance. Key areas of change would include strengthened representation in the senior leadership of the IMF, World Bank and World Trade Organisation. Similarly, large Asian developing countries will need to play a greater part in international standards-setting bodies such as the Basel Committee, although some steps have already been taken in this direction since the creation of the G-20.

This increasing economic weight in the global economy will also bring new responsibilities for Asia. Industrialised Asian countries that exit the ranks of the low-income developing countries will need to ramp up their involvement of development assistance to other developing countries.

Within the Asia-Pacific, the need for new financial and economic architecture becomes increasingly evident. ASEAN has provided an important forum for regional cooperation. Amongst the ASEAN member countries, ASEAN has already proven to be an increasingly valuable regional grouping for its member countries for political and economic cooperation. The achievements in the trade liberalisation agenda with the ASEAN Free Trade Agreement have been a notable milestone, with planning for an ASEAN Economic Community providing a vision for closer economic cooperation. There has been significant progress towards an Asian regional financial architecture through the ASEAN+3 Chiang Mai Initiative and its subsequent evolution. Eventually, Asian regional financial cooperation could evolve into an Asian Monetary Fund.

On the political front, there are a multitude of regional flashpoints, including territorial disputes between China and India over Arunachal Pradesh, as well as between India and Pakistan over Kashmir. Other geopolitical flashpoints in the Asia-Pacific include the Korean peninsula and the South China Sea.

It would therefore be important and timely for a regular mechanism for regional political, economic and financial cooperation to be created in Asia. There are signs of the early beginnings for such dialogue. The new ASEAN Defence Ministers Plus with Eight Dialogue Partners forum (ADMM+), which was established by ASEAN in October 2010, and the ASEAN Regional Forum (ARF), could become the building blocks and key platforms for regional dialogue on defence and security issues.

As Winston Churchill stated in a speech given at Harvard University in 1943 while serving as British Prime Minister during the Second World War, strong international institutions have an important role to play in maintaining peace and preventing conflict.

"We have learned from hard experience that stronger, more efficient, more rigorous world institutions must be created to preserve peace and to forestall the causes of future wars." Prime Minister Winston S. Churchill, 6th September 1943, "The Price of Greatness", Speech at Harvard University.

A key challenge for Asia in the next decade will be to create such strong institutions for Asia-Pacific regional, political and economic cooperation, to preserve the peace and prevent regional conflict.

Future Asia

There has been immense economic progress in the Asia-Pacific over the last fifty years, as rapid economic growth has lifted hundreds of millions out of extreme poverty. A number of Asian nations have succeeded in transforming their economies into advanced economies with high average living standards. These Asian miracle economies are Japan, South Korea, Taiwan, Hong Kong and Singapore.

However, the driving force that is reshaping the balance of global economic power from West to East is the rise of China, as its population of 1.2 billion people move out of poverty and into the ranks of the middle class. India, which is also a nation of 1.2 billion people, is further behind on its development path than China, but will also be contributing significantly to the tidal wave of consumer-led growth that will change the shape of the global economy over the next three decades.

The economic ascent of such large nations as economic powers will inevitably bring increasing global competition for scarce resources, such as oil and gas, coal, metals, agricultural commodities and water. Other dimensions of increasing global competition will be in wars for technological leadership and rivalry between multinationals for global markets.

The key to the geopolitical implications of such transformational change in the Asia-Pacific will be in whether Asia-Pacific governments can harness the benefits of rapid economic growth to build regional peace and cooperation or whether it will lead to political rivalry, military arms races within the Asian region and heightened potential for conflict.

The Asia-Pacific region currently stands at the crossroads in its choices. If the governments of the Asia-Pacific region do not embark on a determined programme of building the regional architecture for political, security and economic cooperation, then the risk of future conflicts in regional geopolitical flashpoints remains a threat to Asia's sustained path of economic progress and human development. Indeed, the Asia-Pacific may already be at the brink of a regional arms race.

However, if the platforms for greater regional cooperation can successfully be built, the 'Asian Century' can be Asia's golden age, with hundreds of millions more lifted out of poverty and the Asia-Pacific region becoming an increasingly powerful driving force for global economic growth.

Bibliography

Ackroyd, P., *Venice Pure City*. [Chatto & Windus] (London, 2009)

Bayly, C.A & Harper, T.N, *Forgotten Wars: The End of Britain's Asian Empire*. [Penguin] (USA, 2008)

Blake, R., *Jardine Matheson: Traders of the Far East*. [Weidenfeld & Nicolson] (London, 1999)

Blood, Peter ed. *Pakistan: A Country Study*. [GPO for the Library of Congress] (Washington, 1994)

Clinton, B., *My Life*. [Hutchinson] (New York, 2004)

Clutterbuck, R., *The Long, Long War: The Emergency in Malaya 1948–60* [Cassel & Co] (1966)

Cohan, W.D., *The Last Tycoons*. [Penguin Books] (London, 2008)

Dikotter, F., *Mao's Great Famine*. [Bloomsbury] (London, 2010)

Enright, M.J., & Hoffmann W.J., *China into the Future: Making Sense of the World's Most Dynamic Economy*. [Wiley] (Singapore, 2008)

Farrell, B.P., *The Defense and Fall of Singapore 1940–42* [Tempus Publishing] (Stroud, 2005)

Field Marshal Slim, W., *Defeat into Victory*. [Cassell] (London, 1956)

Galbraith, J.K., *A Short History of Financial Euphoria*. *[Penguin]* (USA,1993)

Giegerich, B., *Europe and Global Security*. [Routledge] (Oxon, 2010)

Greenspan, A., *The Age of Turbulence: Adventures in a New World*. [Penguin] (USA, 2007)

Hall, J.W., *Japan: From Prehistory to Modern Times*. [Tuttle Publishing] (Germany, 1968)

Hart, A.F and Jones, B.D., *How Do Rising Powers Rise? Survival Vol. 52 no.6, IISS*, (Dec. 2010–Jan. 2011)

Hill, D., *The Gold Rush*. [William Heinemann] (Australia, 2011)

Hobsbawm, E.J., *Industry and Empire*. [Pelican Books] (Great Britain, 1968)

Holslag, J., *Trapped Giant: China's Military Rise*. IISS. [Routledge] (Oxon, 2010)

Howard, J., *Lazarus Rising*. [Harper Collins] (Australia, 2010)

Hughes, J., *The End of Sukarno: A Coup That Misfired: A Purge That Ran Wild*. [Archipelago Press] (New York, 1967)

Indonesia: The First 50 Years, 1945–1995. *[Archipelago Press]* (New York, 1995)

Jalan, B., *India's Politics: A View from the Back Bench*. [Penguin & Viking] (New Delhi, 2007)

James, L., *Raj: The Making of British India*. [Abacus] (London, 1998)

Kissinger, H., *On China*. [Penguin Press] (New York, 2011)

Koch, C.J., *The Year of Living Dangerously*. [Penguin Books] (New York, 1983)

Krugman, P., *The Return of Depression Economics and the Crisis of 2008* [W.W Norton & Company] (New York, 2009)

Lyman R., *Slim, Master of War Burma and the Birth of Modern Warfare*. [Robinson] (London, 2004)

Magnus, G., *Uprising: Will Emerging Markets Shape or Shake the World Economy?* [Wiley] (Chichester, 2011)

Mahbubani K., *The New Asian Hemisphere*. [Public Affairs] (New York, 2008)

Mandela, N., *The Autobiography of Nelson Mandela Long Walk to Freedom*. [Back Bay Books/Little, Brown and Company] (New York, 1994)

Moller, J.O., *How Asia Can Shape the World: From the Era of Plenty to the Era of Scarcities*. [ISEAS Publishing] (Singapore, 2011)

Myint, H., *Economic Theory and the Underdeveloped Countries*. [Oxford University] (London, 1971)

Office of the Director of National Intelligence, *Global Water Security, Intelligence Community Assessment, ICA 2012–08* (USA, February 2012)

Overtveldt J.V., *Bernanke's Test, Ben Bernanke, Alan Greenspan and the Drama of the Central Banker*. [Agate] (Chicago, 2009)

Prestowitz, C., *Three Billion New Capitalists, The Great Shift of Wealth and Power To The East*. [Basic Books] (New York, 2005)

Reinhart, C.M. & Rogoff, K.S., *This Time Is Different: Eight Centuries of Financial Folly*. [Princeton University Press] (Princeton, 2009)

Roach, S.S., *The Next Asia: Opportunities and Challenges For a New Globalization*. [Wiley] (New Jersey, 2009)

Rogers, J., *Investment Biker: Around the World With Jim Rogers*. [Wiley] (Chichester, 2000)

Rostow W.W., *The Stages of Economic Growth: A Non-Communist Manifesto*. [Cambridge University Press] (London, 1960)

Sachs, J., Bono., *The End of Poverty: How We Can Make It Happen in Our Lifetime*. [Penguin] (London, New York, 2005)

Sanyal, S., *The Indian Renaissance: India's Rise after a Thousand Years of Decline*. [Penguin & Viking] (New Delhi, 2008)

Schwartz, D.J., *The Magic of Thinking Big*. [Thorsons] (London, 1984)

Seymour, W., *British Special Forces*. [Grafton Books] (London 1986)

Smith, C., *Singapore Burning: Heroism and Surrender in World War II*. [Penguin] (London, 2005)

Soros, G,. *The New Paradigm for Financial Markets*. [Perseus Books Group] (New York, 2008)

Soros, G., *The Crash of 2008 and What It Means*. [Perseus Books Group] (New York, 2008)

Taleb, N.N., *Fooled by Randomness: The Hidden Role of Chance in Life and in the Markets*. [Penguin Books] (London, 2004)

Tariq A., *The Nehrus and the Gandhis*. [Picador] (London, 1985)

Thant, Myint-U, *Where China Meets India: Burma and the New Crossroads of Asia*. [*Faber and Faber*] (London, 2011)

Thompson, J. *Ready for Anything: The Parachute Regiment at War*. [Fontana] (London, 1990)

US Department of Defense, *Annual Report to Congress: Military and Security Developments Involving the People's Republic of China 2012*. (Office of the Secretary of Defense, May 2012)

Vogel, Ezra, *Japan as Number One*. [Harvard University Press] (Cambridge, Mass., 1979)

Von Tunzelmann, A., *Indian Summer: The Secret History of the End of an Empire*. [Pocket Books] (London, 2007)

Warren, A., *Singapore 1942: Britain's Greatest Defeat*. [Talisman] (London, 2002)

Webster, D., *The Burma Road*. [Pan Books] (New York, 2003)

Welsh, F., *A History of Hong Kong*. [Harper-Collins] (London, 1994)

Yew, L.K., *From Third World To First: The Singapore Story: 1965–2000* [*Times Media Private*] (Singapore, 2000)

Yoong, L.Y., *ASEAN Matters*. [World Scientific Publishing Co] (Singapore, 2011)

Index